WHAT'S IT
ALL ABOUT
RALPHIE?

WHAT'S IT ALL ABOUT RALPHIE?

MY STORY

Ralph Milne

with

Gary Robertson

BLACK & WHITE PUBLISHING

First published 2009
by Black & White Publishing Ltd
29 Ocean Drive, Edinburgh EH6 6JL

1 3 5 7 9 10 8 6 4 2   09 10 11 12

ISBN: 978 1 84502 269 3

The publisher has made every reasonable effort to contact
copyright holders of images in the picture section. Any errors are
inadvertent and anyone who, for any reason, has not been contacted
is invited to write to the publisher so that a full acknowledgment
can be made in subsequent editions of this work.

A CIP catalogue record for this book is available from the British Library.

Typeset by Ellipsis Books Limited, Glasgow
Printed and bound by MPG Books Ltd, Bodmin, Cornwall

CONTENTS

ACKNOWLEDGEMENTS

I'll start with the two most important people who brought me into this world and gave me life – my mum and dad – hopefully I made you both proud. Thank you also to my sister Linda and brothers George and Keith for the special family bond we had and still have. You are forever in my heart.

To my sons Bradley and Robert – you both made a father very proud and I love you always. Thanks to all my family and friends who have supported me through thick and thin, good times and bad, you mean the world to me.

Special thanks to a very special friend indeed – Andy, we go back a long, long way mate! Bill Donaldson and Dundee Celtic Boys Club for giving me a start in football and many happy memories. Thanks to Dundee United Football Club for giving me the opportunity and to all ex-staff and team mates whom I regard as 'family'. Stan Frew and Mrs Lindsay, two Tannadice legends. To everyone I've met during my career and beyond, too many to mention by name but you've all connected with me, even if it was just briefly. Thanks to Black & White for giving me this opportunity to tell my story and to all of you who read it.

Finally, sincere thanks to you Gary and also to your wife and children for showing the utmost patience whilst allowing you the time to do this. You are a true Arab and trusted friend. It has been an incredible path and I cannot thank you enough – Cheers – your friend for life . . .

Ralph

Firstly, I would like to thank my beautiful wife Sue and children Cailean and Eilidh for supporting me wholeheartedly whilst I buried my head in 'writing isolation' for some seven months to work with Ralph. Without your love and inspiration I could not carry on doing something which I have grown to love. Also, the kind words of support and encouragement from family and friends, you know who you are. It means a lot to me and keeps me reaching for that light at the end of the tunnel when I'm in danger of crumbling with 'cabin fever'!

Special thanks to Davie and Sandra Young of Fintry for encouraging a 'scheme boy' to keep going. Truly, you'll never know how much your unwavering support and enthusiasm helped pull me through some tough days.

The books *Rags To Riches* by Mike Watson and *Dundee United – Champions of Scotland 1982-83* by Peter Rundo proved invaluable as back-up when checking facts and figures, and Jim McLean's *Jousting With Giants* (Mainstream, 1987) is a fascinating read by one of Britain's finest-ever managers, as you can see in the short extracts here.

I'm very grateful to Bill Donaldson and all of Ralph's ex-team mates who kindly gave up their time and allowed me

ACKNOWLEDGEMENTS

to interview them – much appreciated lads! Thanks also to
Big Al for those phone calls and texts which kept me right.

A massive bundle of thanks to Campbell Brown, Alison
McBride and all at Black & White Publishing for taking the
book on and believing in it.

Lastly, thanks to you Ralph. It has been a very great pleasure,
honour and privilege to work with you and personally get to
know the man and legend that I so passionately cheered for
from the Tannadice terraces back in the heyday.

Many thanks to D C Thomson of Dundee, Dave Martin at
Fotopress, *The Daily Record*, Peter Rundo, Frank Tocher, South
London Tangerines and any others we may have forgotten
who kindly gave their permission for use of their photographs.

Gary

FOREWORD
BY ANDY 'PITS' McPHEE

I was born in 1961, in Douglas, Dundee – the same year as the boy who lived only three doors away from me. We struck up a great friendship very early on and to this day we have remained lifelong friends. Ralph Milne and I attended different schools, he being a Protestant and me a Catholic, but it gives me great satisfaction knowing that religion was never an issue with regards to our friendship and growing up through our childhood.

It was only a matter of time before Ralph would be recognised in the local football scene as he possessed what can only be described as 'exceptional talent'. We were both involved from a very young age with Dundee Celtic Boys Club, playing Under-11s to Under-14s, and travelled to Kirkton every Thursday for training. Unfortunately, I was not up to the standard of the 'Charleston and Lochee Mafia' and was rarely included in the squad for those Sunday games. Getting a wee bit fed up of this, I informed Ralph I was packing it in. At that time Ralph was kingpin at the club and was scoring a huge number of goals every season, so when I let Ralph know what my intentions were, in typical Ralph Milne fashion, he approached the manager at that time and said, 'If Andy McPhee doesn't get a game then I'm leaving Celtic Boys!'

To my amazement and sheer joy I was named in the starting eleven for the next game at Camperdown Park in Dundee. Sadly, my jubilation was short-lived for our intended opponents didn't turn up and that was that, my big chance had gone! The point I'm trying to make is; here was a fourteen-year-old boy taking on the high and mighty of Celtic Boys and who was prepared to sacrifice his own position just so his mate could get a game! Because this lad from Douglas had speed and skill and an outstanding ability to score goals, the management discreetly bowed to the demands being made by young Milne. I think this action by Ralph indicates how stubborn and loyal he could be when it came to his friends, but also shows how he was prepared to stand up to authority when he felt the need.

In 1977, George and Mabel Milne were the proudest parents in Balunie Drive, Douglas, when they realised their youngest child had just signed professional with Dundee United FC. Football records tell the true story of what followed, none more so than the record which Ralph holds to this day as Dundee United's top European goalscorer. This is a record I personally think will never be beaten. And of course every United fan who witnessed the Championship team of 1983 must remember the lift and the anticipation the crowd got whenever he had the ball at his feet.

After his Tannadice days Ralph moved down south to pastures new, this you will read about in the following chapters. Ralph Milne made a lot of people proud; his family, his neighbours and his pals. So from a pal who would play two-touch in St Pius School playground to a Dundee United legend who terrorised the elite in Europe – 'Cheers and well done.'

'Pits'

INTRODUCTION
BY GARY ROBERTSON

Before Ralph tells his story, I wanted to tell you how this book came about. It was Saturday 8 November 2008 in the 4Js Bar, Dundonald Street, Dundee – the nearest watering hole to Tannadice Park, home of Dundee United Football Club. A few hours had passed since the final whistle had blown signalling the end of the match between United and their bitter north-east rivals Aberdeen. United had won 2 1 and, in doing so, sent their fans into tangerine delirium. Many, like myself, headed for the bar to celebrate with friends and analyse the whole ninety minutes of action and convince ourselves that 'yes, we are the *greatest* team in the world!' The brilliant atmosphere which fills the place when the team wins (especially against Aberdeen!) was clearly evident and every now and then the clientele would erupt into a victory chorus of *Jimmy Gomis* or *Glory Glory Dundee United*. Then the doors swung open and in poured a large group of men who were smartly dressed in sharp suits and overcoats. These were the guys who had just enjoyed the 'free' drink from the Tannadice hospitality package and were looking to carry on the festivities. I didn't know initially, but soon would, that an ex-United legend from the 1983 League-winning side was among that group.

I was a wee bit worse for wear when a friend said to me, 'There's Ralphie Milne.' I admit I had to ask him which guy it was in the throng of bodies. I had never set eyes on Ralph since he left Dundee United nearly twenty-two years ago and his appearance had obviously changed since then. Seeing someone whom I, along with thousands of others, regard as a Dundee United living legend, standing in the same pub only ten feet away had a somewhat strange but exciting effect on me. I have to admit I was a little bit awestruck. This was the man whom I'd watched from the terraces totally annihilate defences with a turn of speed and ball control which I had witnessed in no other. His uncanny habit of scoring truly spectacular goals was the cue to send the 'tangerine legions' into doing 'The Shed Boy's Dance' and more often than not, many of us would get trampled underfoot in the sways, but hell – it was worth it! On 14 May 1983 I watched from the enclosure behind Jim McLean's dugout as Ralph chipped Dundee keeper Colin Kelly to open the scoring with what can only be described as an 'insane effort'. United went on to win the Scottish Premier Division and Ralph and the rest of the squad had their names etched into club folklore for eternity.

I'd be lying if I said I hadn't heard stories of Ralph's liking for a beer or two, or more, but unless these stories are coming from the horse's mouth then they can only be taken for what they really are – rumours! Only Ralph can tell the true story. And so it was, completely by chance, I was drawn into his company by another acquaintance and introduced to him and his friend Andy McPhee. We chatted briefly about his football career and of the book I'd written about the Dundee gangs. He then said, 'I'd like to write a book about my life.' Right away I told him he should and that he no doubt had one hell of a story to tell. He then put it to me, 'Why don't we work together and do it?' I didn't even hesitate and answered, 'OK, if you're up for it, we'll do it.' The fact I was halfway through work on another book didn't matter at all. I told him I was willing to put everything else aside in order to work whole-heartedly on this project. He said simply, 'I'll tell you every-thing, warts and all.' We did the customary spit on the hand and shook on it there and then. Andy ordered up a bottle of champagne and we toasted getting down to work on the book. After a good few rounds we left the 4Js and got a taxi down to Ralph's local, Doc Ferry's in Broughty Ferry, where the party continued. As we parted company at the end of a great night we assured each other that this wasn't just 'drink talking' and the game was definitely on.

True to his word, Ralph phoned me on the Sunday morning to discuss when we were going to get started. Even though my head was pounding this was exactly what I needed to hear and I knew then that Ralph was committed. Over the course of some seven months we got together to conduct countless interviews in the comfort of Doc Ferry's and Papa Jacques and I listened intently as he laid out all his cards on the table. From a personal point of view, it was an honour and privilege to hear the remarkable story unfold of someone whom I regard as one of the finest football players I've ever had the pleasure of watching. Ralph was no run-of-the-mill orthodox player and his sometimes controversial off-field actions have mirrored some of the true greats who have gone before him and who will continue to do so in the future. He chose to do things his way and it is inevitable with a story like this that some feathers are going to be ruffled along the way. Not everyone is going to enjoy reading this book but he never set out with the intention of writing it to gain any pats-on-the-back or gathering of Brownie points in the first place. Nor did he go out of his way to crucify anyone in the process. This is Ralph Milne, pure and simple. Hopefully you will enjoy reading it as much as I have enjoyed working with a man who was a true footballing legend of his era.

FOR RALPHIE

83

Great expectations, September 82
Could this be the season, wen the Arab dream come true?
A team o hardened warriors, stood riddee fir the fray
Braced fir a campaign waged on turf, thit wid rage right
    through tull May
Rez rez ye Tangerines, lit the terrace voice be heard
Tribal chants ten-thoozand strong, beltin oot fae the Cliff an
    the Shed
The Arab Army wiz amassed, the scene wiz set the play wiz
    cast
Fir fathers, sons, eh the weemin an ah – the memories lang
    wid last

Furst blood tih United, an Aiberdeen scalped
Lambs tih the slaughter, the sheepshaggers wahlupt
Jist the furst o many, thit wid taste the Arab guns
Fae the Hibees tih the Killie, fae the Celtic tih the Huns
Fevs, sixes, seevins – a Tangerine rampage
The Terrors runnin riot, United's goalden age
Anither European conquest, fae PSV tih Prague
Once again the did us proud, as the flew the saltire flag

Then wen the needed bottle – the proved the hud it ah
Pittodrie, March o 83, it wiz backs against the wah
2-1 up wi ten men, the jist managed tih hing on
It wiz now atween United, the Glezgae Celtic an the Dons
Performed even mair heroics, second visit tih Celtic Park
Doon tih ten men yit again, the silenced the Jungle's bark
Wi the gemme poised at 2-2, Eamonn Bannon ripped doon
    the weeng
Then Ralphie lobbed Pat Bonner – mibbee it wizna jist a
    dream!

An so tih the grand finale – the final scene o the play
May 14 1983 – Dens Park, oh wut a day!
As tension fuhled the air, the gladiators entered the ring
The Tangerine Legions erupted, the whole toon musta heard
    thum sing
Six minutes in Ralphie's through, an Kelly's aff eez line
As the ba floats ower eez napper, itz a moment caught in
    time
BANG! The ba hits the back o the net, an maist o the grund
    explode
But the Arabs irna feenished yit, the set thir sites an then
    reload
Big Narey gits drapped in the box – 'Penalty!' nae questions
    asked
Up steps Bannon wi nerves o steel, ee puhlz the trigger hard
    then blasts
Colin Kelly maks the save, but ee canna stop Eamonn boy
The net gits rattled again, an the fans go wild wi joy
Quaater-tih-fev it feenished 2-1, an the Dens Derry wir seeck

RALPHIE

Especially wen MacFarlane's words wir remembered – 'the
forlorn hope's' won the League!
Half the toon went right on the pish, the ither half mumped
an girned
While Pat Reilly smiled fae the stars, eez wee team wir
champs confirmed
United, Scotland's Number One, guided beh the great
McLean
Raise yir glesses, pye homage tih they legends, here's the roll-
call o that team . . .

McAlpine, Starky, Malpas, Goughie, Heggie, Narey, Bannon,
Milne, Kirky, Luggy, Doddsy, Holty, Reilly
An tih the ithers wah helped alang the weh – we salute yiz
all!

Gary Robertson

1

A DOUGLAS BOY

I came into this world kicking and screaming in Dundee's Maryfield Hospital at 10.10pm on 13 May 1961. When I was old enough to understand, I was told that *Sportscene*, surprisingly enough, had just come on telly when my proud dad received the joyful news that mum had given birth to a healthy wee boy. On hearing this he promptly marched over to Mr and Mrs Mackay's, the neighbours' house and proclaimed, 'he's here!' then purposefully announced, 'I'm going away to phone Scott Symon (the then Rangers manager) and tell *him* he's here.' Dad had a wee soft spot for the Gers back then.

Home for me, the newest addition to the Milne's, was a terraced house in the large council housing scheme of Douglas, situated at the eastern end of Dundee. Our house was just down from the infamous Lea Rig pub. Being the youngest of four, I was very much fussed over and cared for by my two older brothers Keith and George and my sister Linda. Along with my parents we shared a very close-knit family and as a bright-eyed little lad I absorbed anything and everything I could from them. I felt extremely privileged as a youngster to have such a special relationship with my family and the

1

knowledge I gained subsequently held me in good stead when I attended the nearby Douglas Primary School. Within a couple of months my parents were contacted by the headmaster who wished to push me forward a year due to my academic advancement. The fact I was a year younger than my fellow classmates mattered not and I soon began to excel in my class work. This was only made possible thanks to that early grounding by my family.

Dad was a real character who commanded respect. He was only 5ft 2in tall but not one to be crossed, that's for sure. I had a very special bond with him though, a brilliant man. He had served his country in the Second World War with the famous 'Eighth Army' and was a part of the elite band of men we know nowadays as the SAS. He told us one of his jobs was to blow up bridges and to do this he was expected to hold his breath underwater for around seventy seconds, whilst planting high explosives. Latterly he worked for the Sunblest bakery in Lytton Street, Dundee, now long since gone.

My grandfather on dad's side was a military man as well and had served in the First World War. He was given a sword by a woman whose husband had carried it during the Boer War, which was later passed on to my uncle Ralph. Another uncle, Ralph's older brother Stanley, was unfortunately injured severely in an explosion at work in a factory in Monifeith and lost his right arm. Incredibly, he drove a manual car for the rest of his life with only one arm. He also made a large shield to go with the sword for my grandfather. Both these items are now with my uncle Ralph in Natick near Boston, Massachusetts, where he has lived for years.

Uncle Ralph and Auntie Joan both played the drums in a pipe band and I remember being taken up to the Braemar

Gathering to watch them. The journey was a nightmare and I spewed up in the car, probably after stuffing too many sweets into my mouth. When my granddad passed away it was my first experience of a death in the family and I remember the circumstances in which I was told very clearly. It was the morning of Hogmanay (New Year's Eve) and the house was briefly empty when the phone rang. A voice came on and explained she was from the care home then asked for my dad but I explained there was no one in and asked if I could take a message. She said, 'Can you let Mr Milne know that his dad has died please?' then she put the phone down. I was completely shocked. My dad came in from the shops a few minutes later, saw the look on my face and asked what was wrong. I just broke down when I tried to tell him the news. Even after all these years I still find it utterly cold and without compassion the way they conveyed that news to us. We were due to travel through to my older brother's house in Edinburgh to celebrate New Year and later on my dad decided we would still go as he didn't want to let the family down.

My mum was quite a religious woman and, like most mums, worked her socks off looking after the four of us and keeping the house in order. She also worked casually for DC Thomson's and for the Co-op to bring some extra money into the house.

I really enjoyed school life and my early primary days saw me either second top or top of the class. More often than not though I had to settle for second because there was this bloke who was a right smart-arse! I must confess though, I was no squeaky clean angel and did get the belt occasionally during my school days. As well as the academic side I loved sport and football in particular. As far back as I can remember I was kicking a ball or anything that even resembled the shape of a ball. For me, football was everything. I played it with a passion, as did my mates, and we were all totally consumed by it. In the school playground we would commandeer the shed for games of 'headers' and as soon as the final bell rang you had a ball at your feet again. It could be a tennis ball, anything, it really didn't matter. Tea was then scoffed rapidly and you were back out organising a game and playing till the last possible moment before a 'thick ear' was administered by an irate mum!

When I was learning piano my dad used to phone his mate up in Lochee and tell him to listen while I plinked and plonked my way through Amazing Grace. Coming from a working-class background, learning piano or any other instrument for that matter was never really socially acceptable amongst my peers but I quite enjoyed music. I was actually not too bad on the old Joanna but had to give up lessons due to a lack of family funds and, of course, my huge interest in football.

As a youngster I never went to watch much football, I always preferred to play it. My first ever match, believe it or not, was to see Dundee play Aberdeen which my dad took me to. As for United, I never saw the first team play until I was actually with them. For those readers who don't know, the city has two clubs – Dundee FC, who play at Dens Park, and Dundee United, who play at Tannadice Park. These grounds are a stone's throw from each other, the closest of any in Britain and enjoy the usual derby rivalry whenever they're playing in the same league. Dundee were the more dominant of the two for many years and had their most successful period during the 1960s, winning the old Division One in 1962 and reaching the semis of the European Cup the following year. Dundee United appointed Jim McLean (who, incidentally, was coach of Dundee FC at the time) as new manager in 1971, an appointment which would eventually see the tables of success turned.

At the end of the 1960s and into the early 70s, gang warfare was a big problem in the city and affected most, if not all, of the housing schemes. The local gang where I lived were known as the TODDY and would guard the scheme's boundaries with all the passion and pride of a street tribe. On other occasions they would go team-handed onto a rival scheme's turf or into town knowing full well there was a high chance of aggro from some like-minded mob of youths. The Dundee gangs had a unique form of identification – coloured jumpers and cardigans with a separate coloured band going across the chest – and would proudly parade around in these looking like a small army. The TODDY guys congregated at the local shops in their black and blue jumpers, Sta-prest trousers and Doc Marten boots, looking mean and menacing. These were dangerous times to be wandering off into other schemes but, thankfully, I never encountered any trouble and was never involved in the gang scene, nor were any of my older brothers. For me, I was too busy kicking a ball about the streets and the whole thing passed me by.

On the whole, life in the scheme was mostly fun and, boys being boys, we did get up to various acts of mischief and skulduggery. When I was eleven years old my cousin and I were caught drinking alcohol at my auntie's house in Fintry. I didn't see it as a big deal and merely classed it as dabbling in one of the vices of the adult world. Many youngsters in the housing schemes were experimenting with alcohol at the time and I'm sure it's no different nowadays. A couple of years later I learned how to make home brew from a kit.

We used to go up to my friend Gordon's house every week to play table tennis and things. He and his brother were looked after by their grandfather who ran the Ascot Bar in the Westport. One day we were messing around and decided to make some home brew – well rather a lot actually! We got it all bottled and posed it in his granddad's wardrobe. Three weeks later we would all be enjoying the fruits of our labour. Unfortunately, I'd put too much sugar in it to make it stronger and the whole lot exploded with corks flying off like rockets. My mate told me the poor old guy thought that World War Three had kicked off and his house was under attack from some enemy bombers!

Another funny episode happened at that same friend's house when a few of us decided we were going to raise budgies. The plan was to breed them and then sell them on for a tidy little profit, or so we thought! Bizarre as it sounds, we set to work on our project and started gathering material to build an aviary. We nicked a load of 'greenie poles' (washing line poles) for the frame and other bits and pieces from the closies in Craigie. We even acquired the wire netting from some-where and with everyone mucking in we soon had a construc-tion which resembled an aviary. Our budgie club then trotted off into town, clubbed our milk money together and bought about eight budgies. We gave them time to settle into their new home while we had a couple of drinks. Next morning I received a phone call from my mate. 'You better get your arse up here quick.'

'Why, what's happened?' I asked.

'The budgies are all dead,' he replied. Sure enough, when I got up there they were all lying on the deck, KO'd. As we were all new to the budgie-rearing game we didn't realise that an overnight temperature of minus six in the middle of December would have an adverse effect on our little flock!

A lot of people who watched me play football thought I was a natural left-footed player, but I was actually the opposite. I used to spend countless hours in the grounds of St Pius Primary School kicking the ball against a wall with my left foot, over and over, perfecting the necessary control needed with my 'bad foot' till it became second nature. It was just something I did instinctively and the long hours of solo training and forced 'keepie-ups' on the left paid massive dividends in the years that followed.

As any young lad who ever had aspirations of becoming a footballer will tell you, getting a call-up for the school team is something special. It's usually the first step on the ladder for many a professional career. We were lucky and had some great players at Douglas which produced a very successful period for the school. Even as a young player I possessed a 'winning mentality' and hated losing. I wouldn't say I was a bad loser, I just wanted to win so much and that went for anything I did. I remember one primary schools' sports day at Caird Park and we were competing in the 4 x 100 metres sprint. I was running last, holding anchor and when the baton was passed to me we were already three metres up on the rest. I just took off like a rocket and was totally amazed when I glanced around at the end. The opposition were nowhere to be seen – we absolutely demolished them! I was built for speed and this ability to run at pace was a tremendous attribute to take onto the football field.

Andy McPhee was my best pal during those early days and I suppose it's testament to a true friendship that we continue that special bond to this day. Like me, he loved playing football and was as keen as hell but lacked, shall we say, the finer skills of the beautiful game. Both of us used to make the journey to Camperdown Park at the other end of town every Sunday and assemble with the rest of the Dundee Celtic Boys team. We had a cracking outfit and were one of the dominant forces of Sunday boys football in the city, winning trophies year in, year out. I scored over 500 goals in six seasons and thoroughly enjoyed my football with them.

However, there was one small problem which gradually became a big problem and was beginning to eat away at me – Andy was turning up religiously but wasn't being picked for the team. Things came to a head one morning and I just said to the manager, 'That's it; I'm getting sick of this. I'm not coming back unless Andy gets a game!'

Luggy (Paul Sturrock) was coaching us at the time and couldn't believe what he was hearing. 'What are you saying Ralph? Don't be silly, you can't do this!'

I told Luggy exactly the same, that I wasn't coming back unless Andy got a game. I received some reassurance from the coaching staff and so we turned up the next week, Andy full of excitement at the possibility of his first game for the club. Sure enough, there's his name on the team sheet. Standing in the pissing rain we waited and waited. The other team never showed up and bang went Andy's Celtic Boys career! He still laughs about it now. As for Luggy, I can't thank him enough for what he did, not just for me but the rest of the lads as well. He gave up his own free time to come along each week and help with the coaching and pass on valuable tips on how to improve as a player. We all had a huge respect for him and I personally owe a great deal of my early learning to him. To progress in later life and play in what was undoubtedly the greatest Dundee United team ever was uncanny.

I was still doing very well at school and this continued when I went to Craigie High. Again, the main thing for me was sport and getting into the football team. Some time after achieving this, the teacher incredibly began to approach me about team selection and who should play where. I was learning all the time and, even at that young age, I knew where I wanted to go – professional football.

When I reached the age of fourteen I became aware that scouts from some of the senior clubs were turning up at games and watching. There is always a huge burst of adrenaline and heightened anticipation when you know someone is there, possibly casting an eye over you. You're never quite sure if it's for you or not but one thing is certain, you play your socks off, show the correct attitude and commitment and hope to impress enough to secure further interest or even an offer.

Five of us from Dundee Celtic Boys were picked to travel down to Birmingham and train with Aston Villa who were managed at the time by Ron Saunders. We stayed there for a week and were put through our paces, but I hated it. I remember coming home on the train thinking, 'No, I didn't like that place (Birmingham) one little bit'. Four days later I was up in St Columba's school in Downfield when I was approached by the Dundee United manager Jim McLean, Davie Small and Doug Cowie. Wee Jim says, 'I want a word with you.'

'Why, what have I done?' I protested.

'I'm just wondering why you've stopped coming to training?' he asked. Previously, I had been training part-time on Tuesday and Thursday nights with Wattie Smith and Archie

Knox, both of whom were playing for United. Many will know Wattie as the current Glasgow Rangers coach whilst Archie has worked with and assisted some of the best managers in the business. Training with them, however, was murderous. It was all running and physical fitness work and I just couldn't keep up with them, so I jacked it. I answered Jim McLean's question as honestly as I could and told him my reasons for quitting – it was too hard and too tiring, simple as that. I was after all, only a boy who still had to get up for school on the following mornings.

His reply nearly bowled me over. 'I'm only joking,' he said. 'I'm wondering if you would like to sign a contract with us as a schoolboy.'

'Well, I'll need to speak to my dad,' I answered.

'Go and phone your father then.'

I was both excited and cautious when I spoke to my Old Man. 'Dad, I think I'm signing for Dundee United but I'm not sure. They're going to come down to the house to speak to you.' As soon as the phone was down my dad went straight up to the shop next to the Lea Rig and bought a massive carry-out. He put the whole lot on the table and awaited our arrival. God only knows what Jim, Davie and Doug thought when they entered. When I set eyes on this mountain of drink I couldn't believe it!

Wee Jim (McLean) got straight down to business and said, 'Right Mr Milne, this is the way it goes, blah, blah, blah . . . but we need your signature as well.' Dad was chuffed as hell then said, 'Can I offer you guys a wee drink?'

'Oh no, we don't drink Mr Milne!'

I just looked at my dad with a screwed up face and thought 'good one dad!' As soon as they were out the door my dad cracked open his whisky and said 'Congratulations son'. I tried not to laugh when I said, 'Fuck me dad, what was that all about with all that drink?'

'Well, I didn't know did I?' It was my dad's way of showing some polite, working-class hospitality and, although I was a little embarrassed at the time, we were soon laughing our heads off. Seriously though, dad was over the moon that one of his sons had finally made a small, but nonetheless important, breakthrough in the footballing world. He was fairly disappointed when my oldest brother George went to Morgan Academy and they only played rugby. My other brother Keith was a fantastic player but it never happened for him. It was up to me now. I had been given a great opportunity by Dundee United and was damn well going to grab it with both hands!

2

TANGERINE HEAVEN IN 77

The day I signed my schoolboy contract with United it was explained to me that the club would put £3 in a bank account each week and, if they signed me full-time, I would get the accumulative amount. Really though, it was just a load of nonsense because if they decided at the end they didn't want you, then you got nothing. From that moment, whenever I stepped onto a football pitch, I focused all my energy towards my own personal goal and let my feet do the talking.

Around two years later, I left school, which I must confess I absolutely loved. Most of my teachers were very supportive and I have the greatest respect for them and the knowledge they supplied me with. My English teacher was the only one I didn't really hit it off with. He told me I would never pass my English O Grade. Well, I passed all my exams, including an A for English. It's funny but I sometimes think back how things might have been had the football not worked out. That particular summer I spent working with my dad in Sunblest, helping out and earning a few bob. I already knew the place fairly well, having worked a few weekends there when I was thirteen and, as my dad was a gaffer, I had a certain amount of freedom, although you were still expected to graft. He was always taking the mickey out of people and winding them up. Sometimes I couldn't believe the way he'd speak to the guys, but it wasn't done out of nastiness.

When the time came to sign a proper contract with United, I walked out of the bakery, put pen to paper and collected just under £300 from the bank. I was now a professional football player with Dundee United and I was in tangerine heaven!

I was sixteen years old and the year was 1977. The streets of Britain were witnessing a new phenomenon among the country's youth – punk rock! The music was unlike anything that had gone before and shocked parents were up in arms. The Sex Pistols said 'Never Mind The Bollocks', The Clash were having a 'White Riot' and Scotland had gubbed England and made Wembley theirs for the day, borrowing some of the turf in the process.

Having survived a nerve-racking relegation battle in the newly-formed Scottish Premier League the previous year (which saw our great rivals Dundee FC go down on goal difference), United set about turning their fortunes around. They finished fourth and were about to enter the most successful decade in the club's history.

Meanwhile, I had a huge pile of money burning a hole in my pocket. The first thing I did was say to my brother Keith, 'C'mon, we're going for a pint.' We went to the Hansom Cab in the town centre and went right on the bevvy. As we stood scooping he asked me, 'What are you going to do with all that money?'

'I'm going to buy a motorbike!'

His jaw hit the deck. 'What do you want with a motor-bike?'

I told him, 'It's my money and I'm having a bike. And I'm going away down the road to buy mum a radio cassette player.' So that was it, my money was gone just like that. I bought my bike brand new, a Suzuki AP50 from Andrew Hart's up on Milnbank Road. The guy handed me a helmet and a set of keys then left me to it out in the street. I stood there looking at this machine thinking, 'How do you start this thing?' I hopped on, got it started then quickly realised, 'Hey, this thing's a wee bit quicker than me.' I was all over the shop.

I bought the motorbike on the Monday so by the Friday I was feeling like a proper little biker. I was cruising along the Arbroath Road on my way home. It was half-past four and the traffic was really busy. I remember this Harry Lawson lorry coming in the opposite direction and signalling to turn up Dalkeith Road. For some unknown reason I looked in my mirror and thought, 'He's surely gonna cause an accident.' When I glanced forward again I just had a millisecond to register that the Volvo in front of me had braked. Well, nobody damages a Volvo do they! I went straight into the back of it and flew over it. Then I'm lying in the middle of the road thinking, 'What the hell happened there?' Luckily I was only battered and bruised with some rips and tears in my clothes but the bike was mangled with the handlebars now sitting at ninety degrees from their original position. Passengers rushed off a bus and drivers got out of their cars to see if I was OK. I told them I just wanted to get home and, in a somewhat dazed state, I slithered back onto the bike and drove off. It was like a scene from a cartoon!

Wee Jim wasn't too pleased with my new purchase but

there was nothing he could do. I suppose looking back now he should have put his foot down and told me to get rid of it. I had it for about a year and used it whenever I travelled up to Tannadice. Everyone thought I was off my head! Fellow player Graeme Payne told me the funniest thing he ever saw was me taking off down Tannadice Street in a blizzard. The road was plastered with snow and the bike was a wee flier. As I slid and skidded out of sight, he couldn't believe I had managed to stay on. I just laughed and told him it was down to plenty of practice.

My first team debut came in the August of 1977 in a friendly match against Alloa Athletic, but it was to be almost two years before I would repeat this feat and had to content myself with learning my apprenticeship in the reserves. The first senior wage I received was around twenty quid before tax. Prior to this I had been earning a very decent wage doing a milk round and sometimes wished I was back working there when Wee Jim started fining me for what were, at times, ridiculous offences. His fearsome reputation and strict code of discipline I already knew about. However, I didn't feel intimidated by him, you just couldn't. If you did, he'd get to you and you'd be straight out the door. So you had to battle. If you could 'front' him, then you could do it (perform) on the pitch. In saying all that, I wasn't prepared in the slightest for my 'welcome' into senior football and life with the big boys. During my first week there as a full-timer he took us down to the beach at Monifeith. A two-month stay in Hades dragging a ball and chain would have been easier than the hell of that sand! He'd paired all the young players up with two pros that were to look after us during the pre-season training. I teamed up with Frank Kopel and George Fleming.

We kicked off at pace and early on I was already panting and thinking, 'Fuck me, this is hard!' The punishment was relentless, up and down dunes, our lungs screaming out for oxygen. The two rolls which my dad had brought in for me from his nightshift in the baker's were hoyed up. It didn't help either with the gaffer shouting, 'Get up! Get up!' There was no time for any self pity, even though I was still only a boy; I was in a man's world now. When we arrived back at the ground I was still staggering and felt dazed. Wee Jim shouted over to me, 'Ralph, office!' I honestly thought he was about to pull me in and say, 'Well done for keeping going' type of thing. Instead he unleashed a tirade of verbal venom. 'See you ya wee bastard! You *ever* look at me like that again, I'll fine you a week's wages! Don't you ever draw me a dirty look again, you got that?' I was absolutely stunned at what I was hearing, it just didn't make sense. I couldn't even see out of my eyes for the salt and sweat to give *anyone* a 'look', I was so giddy. That, then, was the start of our roller-coaster relationship. Ralph Milne – welcome to Dundee United.

3

IF THE KIDS ARE UNITED

Those early training sessions are memories that will stay with me forever. But they were necessary for what Jim McLean's long-term goals were and what he was trying to achieve with the club. If you look at any great side which has been successful, the two key elements are skill and fitness. Of course, bringing it all together as a team is also vitally important. Before we even kicked a ball at training we were hammered into the ground with some intense and torturous regimes. It was all physical. The benefits though were undeniable and, along with the rest of the lads, I soon became much fitter and stronger.

Wee Jim had begun taking me on the bus, travelling through to the senior games before I went full-time, with the strict instructions 'watch and learn'. I can't fault him for that. It was a clever thing to do. These lessons proved invaluable, not just for my own development, but for all the younger lads. We were after all studying under one of the best tacticians in the game. He was definitely in a class of his own and constantly striving to improve on all levels. However, the bollockings he handed out were something else – and not just to me I may add!

As an S signing I remember one time he accused me of smoking. This was back in the days when smoking was permitted upstairs on the buses and, because I'd gone upstairs with another of the S signings, someone spotted me and automatically assumed that I was smoking. When word got back to the gaffer he pulled me up and asked me the crack. All I could do was protest my innocence and tell him that I hated smoking with a passion but I don't know if he believed me or not. I just couldn't fathom out how his mind worked sometimes. When I was still only sixteen he would phone up my girlfriend's mum to check where I was, making sure I wasn't in the Lea Rig bar. That was just his way and if I wanted to succeed then it was a simple case of 'get the head down and get on with it'. Some of the other younger players were from Edinburgh and staying in digs through here. They also had the pleasure of his nightly phone calls to make sure they were safely tucked up at night and not away out gallivanting.

Since taking over at Tannadice in 1971, McLean's philosophy was to encourage youth development and, together with his scouts, they began to pull in some fantastic home-grown talent as well as others from further afield. In the year I signed, local boy Davie Narey became the first player in United's history to play for Scotland. Others, such as Davie Dodds, John Holt, Billy Kirkwood and Graeme Payne, were either establishing themselves in the United team or would shortly be breaking through. The latter of that particular group was voted Scottish PFA Young Player of The Year for season 1977/78.

Jim McLean's determined policy of honing, nurturing and maturing his young players became the envy of many managers throughout Britain. People were beginning to notice the array of young talent he was blooding in the first team, guys who weren't afraid to mix it with the big boys. As far as he was concerned though, other managers could look but they better not touch! Producing young talent for rival clubs to swan in and poach was not part of his game plan.

For me to be part of this was just tremendous. The more experienced players helped us younger lads fit in and were very supportive. It felt more like a family and the harmony between the players meant everyone was pulling together. I always had the feeling I would force my way into the first team and honestly believed in my ability to make an impact. With all due respect to those around me, I knew the level I was at and where some of the others were at. But it wasn't going to be easy, that's for sure.

The contracts, pay structure and bonus payments which Dundee United operated during Jim McLean's reign have been subject to much debate. Signing as a professional from the schoolboy ranks, you were given a two-year contract. If you showed up well during that period you were offered an extension. When Wee Jim spotted a stand-out he understandably wanted to hold onto them, especially when he had a vision of building a team which would bring success to the club. Having a long-term contract offered a degree of security, but if things went tits up (which they occasionally did) it could be a bit of a nightmare.

My first game for the reserves was against Rangers at Ibrox when I was only fifteen. Their reserve team was like our first team, with loads of big name players. The man given the task of marking me was none other than the legendary figure of John Grieg. By then he was nearing the end of his playing career and wasn't as sharp as he'd been in his heyday.

Unfortunately for me, he still knew how to hit hard. After about ten minutes he booted me right up in the air. When I landed, I just lay there writhing in pain. I thought I was dying! He grabbed me by the back of the neck, picked me up and said, 'Get up Ralph, you're gonna get plenty of that in this game son!' I never went near him after that. He actually scored in that game and we were soundly walloped.

I was to fare much better though in a few reserve matches against Rangers further into my career. During one of these games I was clattered by the tough-tackling Tam Forsyth and lost a boot, but I continued to advance on their goal and chipped their helpless keeper (with my bootless foot) from an absolutely ridiculous angle and watched as the ball sailed into the net. I scored a goal in another game which was very similar to the famous one David Beckham scored for Man United versus Wimbledon. John Reilly was on the run shouting for the pass but as I crossed the halfway line I looked up and saw the Rangers keeper off his line so I just launched it over him and straight into the net.

I remember another reserve match when we played against Brechin City and I scored our only goal. The game finished 1-1 but Wee Jim was not impressed at all, in fact he was severely pissed off. He came into the dressing room and started going round all our numbers one to eleven. I was number eight, I think. 'You're fined a week's wages, you're fined a week's wages' and so on till he came round to me.

'And you're fined a week's wages.'

'I'm not accepting that,' I said.

'What did you say ya wee c***?'

'I said I'm not accepting that.'

'That's two weeks' wages. You got anything else to say?'

'Yes, I'm still not accepting that.'

'That's three weeks' wages. You got anything else to say?'

'Ach fuck off!' He went ballistic after that.

We played Forfar the following week and I scored the winner. He pulled me up at the end and said, 'That's better, I'm only fining you a week's wages!'

As an apprentice at United, myself and the other young lads had certain chores to do, which is par for the course. We had to have the balls, bibs and cones ready for training every morning. Wattie Smith would instruct us on where to set out the cones for routines and we learned a great deal from these training methods. We would take three bags of thirty balls, all of which were old match balls with some nearing their sell-by date. Whilst the senior lads were training, one of these old relics from the twenties went flat and Wee Jim went right off his nut. I think the laces in it had come undone or something! As there were three of us (apprentices), he couldn't point the finger at anyone but it was an incredible over-reaction. I thought, 'Here we go, another week's wages for a ball being flat!'

I was put on kit washing, which I hated. Having felt I'd done my stint for long enough on this particular job I asked Wattie if I could get into the 'boot room' for washing and polishing duties. Wattie obliged but I ended up overstaying my welcome in that department by about three years (I was still polishing the rest of the squad's as well as my own boots before a cup final in the early 80s!). At the time United were sponsored by Adidas but some of the players didn't like these boots and preferred brands like Gola or Puma, purely for comfort. We were given the task of 'blackening' the other brands and painting three white stripes to make them look like Adidas. This was all fine and well until the players started kicking balls and the rain came on – it was comical! I actually became a bit of an artist trying to add the little zigzags onto the stripes.

There were occasions when I used to ask Wee Jim if he'd like his shoes polished before a board meeting. His answer was a blunt 'aye!' There was no 'thanks' or anything remotely polite. He was paid back in kind and I would only polish one shoe. The other was left covered in polish to 'decorate' his nicely pressed flannels. It was daft episodes like these that had me getting him back in my own little ways. It's childish when I think back now but at the time it did give me some satisfaction and reassured me that he wasn't going to get everything his own way, even though he was the boss.

At a time when I really ought to have been maturing, I still couldn't resist the odd bout of mischief and one such bout went slightly out of control. In the cul-de-sac where I lived we had one of those neighbours who liked to have his car parked in the same spot right outside his door. When the space was free I'd sometimes park there for convenience which annoyed our neighbour no end. As soon as I moved it he'd quickly jump in his own car and reclaim *his* space. This began to get on my nerves so one day I went down to the iron-monger's in Castle Street and bought a kilo of the u-shaped nails which they used on fence posts. I got a big elastic band and said to my older brother Keith, 'As soon as I let this go, you close the window and pull the curtain.' I started cracking these nails off the neighbour's window which made a hell of a noise.

I'm ashamed to admit we began to persecute the guy a little and he took to using a pair of binoculars to try and catch the perpetrators. One evening the police chapped the door and I could hear them from upstairs asking my mum if anyone had an air rifle in the house. 'Oh no officer, we don't have any guns in this house!' My mum shut the door and they carried on their enquiries with the other neighbours. I thought I'd better knock it on the head as it was getting serious but the ceasefire didn't last long. Keith and I went out into the garden and started rattling the tenement windows and having a great laugh. Sure enough, we were soon back targeting *Mr Grumpy's* windows and the wind-up continued.

I returned home one night after playing for the reserves against Hibs and couldn't resist a quick volley at the usual window so we pinged off a few rounds and thought no more about it. As I started getting changed to go out for a pint I heard the approaching wail of sirens. I pulled the curtains back and saw *Mr Grumpy's* shed well alight. What we didn't know until later was that the guy was a bit of an alcoholic and he thought whoever was responsible for hitting his windows was hiding in his shed so he torched it! That was the end of the nonsense.

On 28 July 1979, I made what I would consider my proper first team appearance for Dundee United in a pre-season Dryburgh Cup match at Tannadice against Dunfermline Athletic. My memories of that day, apart from it being a monumental occasion in my playing career, were that of Wee Jim going off his nut at half-time, a lot of it directed towards me. He was bawling and shouting that I hadn't followed someone's shot in and so passed up a scoring opportunity. He blasted, 'For every ten you follow in, you'll get one (a goal)!' and he was right. I scored the final goal in a 3-0 win. If I remember correctly he seemed to rant and rave for most of the match. It was intense. As an eighteen-year-old on your debut, you're thinking its all being directed at you, but it wasn't.

I went to Tannadice as a centre forward but United already had Paul Sturrock and Davie Dodds. As I was quicker than both of them, I ended up playing mostly on the right wing. Occasionally I played on the left wing, sometimes in the centre; it all depended on who was fit and who was injured. I didn't mind this. Obviously you want to play centre forward and score all the goals but he (McLean) wasn't going to move Luggy. He got in there first. I had never played in the wing position before. It's a totally different game and you have to adjust accordingly. Admittedly, the speed I had made me an ideal candidate for the wing, but the crossing was something I had to work on.

When I had joined United I was a bit of a lightweight, weighing in around ten stone with a wet donkey jacket on, but with the rigorous training regime, I eventually bulked up. The extra muscle improved my all-round strength and made me shift even faster. I was once timed over a hundred yards wearing normal trainers and clocked up a very impressive 10.1 seconds. Of course, it was great being fast but it was equally important to be able to control, cross, pass and shoot the ball too.

Parkhead was the venue for my League debut and a tussle with the Glasgow giants Celtic. It seems strange but I never felt intimidated going into that game given the personal significance of it. United had been making steady progress over the past three years and the growing confidence within the team meant places like Parkhead and Ibrox were beginning to lose their 'fear factor'. We now at least *felt* we could go to Glasgow and win. This had a huge psychological effect and I relished the prospect of going up against the likes of ex-United man Tom McAdam, Roy Aitken and big Johannes Edvaldsson.

We were getting beat 2-1, one of their goals coming from George McCluskey, which was an absolute cracker. I was sitting on the subs bench when Wee Jim decided to go for broke and threw me on. Our keeper Hamish (McAlpine) launched the ball straight up the middle of the park and I went after it. Their defenders, McAdam and Edvaldsson just kept backing off. I caught the ball sweet off the bounce and fired it from twenty five yards straight into the top corner. We left with a point but, incredibly, Wee Jim was reluctant to give me the bonus saying it was far too much money for a young lad to be having!

My first taste of football against European opponents came just a week or so later in the UEFA Cup when we played Belgian outfit Anderlecht in a disappointing 0-0 draw at home. I sat on the bench but didn't feature in the away leg, a game which was most memorable for Frank Kopel's match-winning twenty-five-yard screamer. I'm sure that was Hamish's first game back since he'd been sent home by the club during the previous end of season tour in Japan. He and Wee Jim had been arguing tactics over where Holty's (John) position should be at corners. Jim wanted him four yards from the post whereas Hamish wanted him six so he had room to come out and punch the ball clear. Next thing they were going at it hammer and tongs, bawling and shouting. A little later our physio Andy Dickson went to Hamish's room and told him to pack up his gear and go home – *from Japan!* Hamish just said, 'Up yours,' and left.

He made his peace with the club during the pre-season but Jim had brought in goalkeepers Peter Bonnetti and John

Gardiner as cover, probably to teach Hamish a wee lesson and provide some competition. Anyway, we were having a practice match with Hamish in one goal, Peter in the other and John Gardiner behind collecting the balls. John chapped Jim's door the next day and said, 'Can I see you a minute boss?'

'Aye, what is it?' he asked.

'I think I'm the best keeper,' claimed John.

Wee Jim was gobsmacked. 'You think you're the best keeper *here?*'

'No, I think I'm the best keeper in the world,' he answered.

'Well you go out there and show me you're the best keeper and I'll put you in the first team.' Next reserve game he came out, missed a cross completely and they scored. Well, none of us knew what had been said previously. Wee Jim stormed into the dressing room at half-time raging, 'You, ya fuckin' big-nosed bastard! You've got the ordocity (he meant audacity!) to come in to my office and tell me you're the *best keeper in the world!*' We're all looking at each other trying not to piss ourselves laughing. After that John was ripped to shreds and slagged off something awful.

Playing for United had brought me back into contact with my very good mate Andy McPhee, who was a huge fan of the club. He had moved to another part of the scheme some years before and we kind of lost touch with each other but one day he phoned up and asked if I could get him a ticket for a forthcoming match. 'No problem,' I said.

'Would you like to go for a pint on Sunday and catch up on tricks?' he asked.

'That would be fine.' We went down the Ferry but back then the only place you could get a drink on a Sunday afternoon was Jolly's pub. We sat there scooping, having a good bevvy when Andy suddenly stopped talking in mid-sentence with a look of anguish on his face then blurted out, 'I've got to go to Mass today!'

'What are you talking about?'

'I've got to go to the chapel. If I don't go my mum will go mental.'

Here we were in the middle of a session and he's got to go to *chapel*? I thought, 'He can't be serious,' but he was. The story took an even more bizarre twist when he announced he'd have to go and pick up his car first which was being repaired by a mechanic in Douglas! In hindsight this was a crazy thing to do, however we did it. We jumped into the car and headed down to St Pius but the street was packed with cars and Andy was beginning to panic. He drove the car right into the church grounds but came to an abrupt halt when he hit a tree.

'Quick, get out, get out!' he shouted. 'No one's clocked us. When we get in here just follow me and do as I do.' As I'm a non-Catholic I didn't have a clue what to expect. I strolled in behind him but was too busy soaking up the beautiful architecture above to notice Andy had dropped down on one knee to engage in some Holy ceremony. I crashed into him and went flying, landing in a heap on the deck, right in front of the priest. Being half-cut I thought this was hilarious and couldn't stop laughing. The whole congregation turned to see what the commotion was as Andy hurriedly pulled me into the pews. I was pissing myself by now – it was sheer Laurel and Hardy comic capers. His mum was only three rows in front of us and one churchgoer was heard saying, 'That's terrible. I'm going to tell that laddie's mum!'

For Dundee United, 1979 was historic with a capital 'H'! I had played in some of the earlier rounds of the Scottish League Cup but didn't get a shout when the team reached the semi or the final. This will sound controversial but, in my opinion, the manager didn't want me to have the bonus payment. For the semi against Hamilton he named his squad and left me out. My place on the bench went to ex-Celtic player Steve Murray who only played two or three times that whole season! The thing was, your bonus was a lot more than what you'd put pen to paper for and the manager was well within his rights to hold you to that contract. Our basic wage was peanuts really, you had to be in the first team to make any money but, in all honesty, playing and being part of the team was way more important than finances. United paid a bonus for a draw and a win. In some games, if both the subs weren't used and the end result was positive, the bonus given to them was only half. It was crazy.

While I'm on the subject of subs, if he put up a first team list of fifteen players, only thirteen could play. He used to say to four of them, 'OK, you four are going to be subs. What do you want to do with the bonus because there are only two bonus payments? Do you want to half it or do you want to keep it for the named players? The players *always* halved it to keep it fair amongst themselves and he really hated that. He wanted guys to be at each other's throats bickering over the payments. We were too solid as a unit though to get involved in crap like that! For the record, the cup final was against Aberdeen at Hampden Park and ended in a forgettable 0-0 draw.

The replay, however, was switched to Dens Park and was a completely different affair. United crushed Alex Ferguson's

Dons 3-0 and so lifted the first major silverware since the club's birth in 1909. I received a medal for playing in the earlier rounds but I would much rather have earned it playing in the final. To Jim McLean's enduring credit, his hard work, focus, devotion and commitment had finally paid dividends and he was hungry for more success. It was a fantastic achievement and fired out a warning shot to the rest of Scottish football – Dundee United were now a force to be reckoned with. It also meant another crack at Europe, something which the fans were almost beginning to expect each season, such was the growing stature of the team.

For me personally, the season 79/80 was the breakthrough into the first team. Although I had only played in a dozen or so games and scored a couple of goals, it was the boost I needed. To cap it all I was awarded 'Reserve Player Of The Year'. The only way from here was up.

4

FROM STRENGTH TO STRENGTH

The 80/81 season kicked off with high hopes of capturing more silverware and hopefully progressing further than the second round in Europe. I remember we began reasonably well but our form dipped a little leading up to the first leg of our UEFA Cup tie, which was away to Polish outfit Slask Wroclaw. The manager took me over with the squad for that one, again I didn't play but the thing that stuck in my mind about the place was the abject poverty. It left quite an impression on me. You just didn't realise how lucky you were till you saw conditions like these. They weren't the worst though; I was to see one or two much darker places during my travels in the coming seasons.

On the subject of Europe, there were a few occasions which followed when I was a wee bit worse for wear prior to travelling for an away tie. Sometimes the club would hire a charter flight and the fans would travel with us, which helped subsidise the costs but other times we didn't have that luxury. One time the squad were told to be suited up and arrive sharp at Tannadice for 5.30am on the Monday morning in order to catch the 7.00am flight from Edinburgh to Heathrow. I always

enjoyed going out for a drink on a Sunday night and sometimes I wouldn't get home until 2.30am. It was a case of power
nap, up, shave, shower and change then down to Tannadice
where I'd sit at the back of the minibus and just about choke
everyone to death with the alcohol fumes. Once I got on and
sat next to Ian Gibson. He turned to me suspecting I'd been
boozing and said, 'Ralph, let me smell your breath?' I nearly
knocked him spark out without even laying a finger on him!

By December 1980 we had reached the final of the League
Cup for the second year in succession. Our opponents were
our arch-rivals from across the road – Dundee. In football
terms this was an historic occasion for the city, especially as
the Scottish football hierarchy had wisely elected to play the
game at Dens Park. This significant gesture meant the fans
were saved the expense and hassle of travelling through to
Hampden Park in Glasgow. The fact it was a derby meant the
stakes were heightened like no other before. Sadly, I was left
out once more and had to settle for cheering the lads on from
the stand. It was a bitter blow but one which I had to accept.
The cup was duly returned to the Tannadice trophy cabinet
as Dundee were demolished by three goals to nil.

There were more off-field shenanigans when I began running
a little ticket scam for gaining entry into The Sands nightclub
in Broughty Ferry. Situated on the Esplanade this was a very
popular venue, especially with the Douglas guys and at weekends wandering eyes would give the 'talent' the once-over.
We (players) were given free passes to the club and the thought
occurred to me that these things could quite possibly be dupli-
cated. My brother owned his own printing business so I asked
him to copy and print some of these passes – well, 500 to be
precise. After a home game it was a case of get out the shower

sharp and bail out for a couple of pints before Wee Jim could pin you down. However, if we were beaten, everyone was kept back for a half-hour grilling. A few of us used to pop up to the Hilltown for a drink in The Plough then off you went home to change into the disco gear and down to Brooks in the Ferry to meet the mates.

It was dodgy having all of these tickets so I used to just take ten or twelve with me each week. Word soon got round though that I had 'free tickets' and the young ladies would approach me enquiring about their availability. Let's just say, the tickets were a great ice-breaker!

With each passing month my confidence and ability on field grew steadily and, with the addition of a good few goals, I felt my senior career was beginning to head in the right direction. Unfortunately, we as a team couldn't build on what had already been a successful season by overcoming Rangers and adding the Scottish Cup too. Prior to reaching that final we had played Motherwell at home in the quarter-finals and annihilated them 6-1. We were five up at half-time and cruising. In all honesty, and with the greatest respect, it could have been ten or twelve. They came out in the second half and made more of an effort and we only managed to score another one goal. The manager came into the dressing room at the end and laid into us full pelt. 'I'm not accepting that second-half performance. You're a bunch of lazy bastards! You're only getting part of the bonus payment!'

He made a proper arse of himself though and went out and told the press he'd fined us. In fact this wasn't correct as the actual bonus sheet stated something different and didn't reflect what he was saying. The press printed the story anyway and Wee Jim was left scratching his head.

If I remember correctly, we went in as slight favourites against Rangers in the final. This time I was given the nod and was included in the starting eleven. We never really got out of first gear though and a largely uneventful match ended 0-0. Rangers dominated the replay and hammered us 4-1 in a hugely disappointing performance from ourselves. Still, the signs were unquestionably positive from a United perspective and when the first ball was kicked heralding the beginning of season 81/82, the mood was one of quiet determination to better the previous achievements. During that summer I went back into the baker's and worked with my dad. This was purely to ease the long weeks without football leading up to our pre-season training.

The campaign began with three rounds of home and away ties in the League Cup which we blazed a trail through with straight wins. Our good form continued and we had the perfect confidence booster at Tannadice in a League match against city rivals Dundee, just four days before our UEFA Cup away tie to French cracks AS Monaco. We dominated, then utterly demolished them 5-2. The scoreline could have been even higher had it not been for the woodwork keeping out a few more efforts. It is a game I fondly recall and remember playing particularly well in, scoring with a sublime chip and generally running amok.

It was the ideal tonic prior to the first *real* test of the season – the difficult first leg in Monaco. At the time Monaco were a very good side but we went over to the little French principality and quite simply ripped them apart. I'm sure the 5-2 scoreline must have echoed around Europe and had the sports journalists talking about this 'little' team from Scotland called Dundee United. On the whole we were still a fairly young side and my own opinion was that this was just the start. There was a feeling in the camp of 'hey wait a minute, we're not a bad side here.'

The next round of that competition saw us drawn against one of the big guns of European football – Borussia Moenchengladbach. The Germans had won the first leg 2-0 and, in typical arrogant fashion, they thought they were coming to Tannadice for a picnic! I scored the first goal to signal the fightback, which eventually turned into a tangerine avalanche and a nightmare for our visitors. The last of the five goals on that night, scored by Eamonn Bannon, was without doubt world class.

Sandwiched between those two Borussia matches we'd managed to secure our third successive League Cup final after disposing of Aberdeen with a 3-0 second leg away win. Our opponents were Rangers whom we'd already beaten at home, this coming during a confidence-boosting winning streak on the back of the hammering of the Germans.

On the Wednesday leading up to the final I'd been on a bit of a bender bevvying and turned up for training the next morning to be greeted by a kangaroo court reception. He (McLean) had gathered a few of the players together and put the question to them, 'Do I play him or not in the cup final?' Now I knew what was going on 'cause I had more spies in there than he did! Admittedly, I was reeking of drink but watched anyway as the group discussed my inclusion or not before training kicked off. Like I say, I'd already twigged what was going on but just readied myself for the coming session.

After a warm-up and some fitness work we got underway with a training match. Wee Jim stood watching from the side-lines as I proceeded to rip the piss out of the whole lot of them. In short, I buried them. Nearly every effort I had on goal went in, goals you just wouldn't expect, left foot, right foot, the lot; it was just one of those days. Wee Jim decided, 'He's in, I'm playing him.' At last I was getting the shout for a League Cup final. But it wasn't to be the fairytale story I'd hoped for.

The form book had us once again as slight favourites going into the match but by half-time the game was still all square at 0-0. I had been getting nothing for those first forty-five minutes, no supply at all. Anyone with even the most basic understanding of football knows a winger needs fed in order to cause damage to an opposing defence. We had just got into the dressing room when over he (McLean) storms and lays right into me. Words were exchanged then he raged, 'I'll punch your pus (face)! You're off, you're off!'

I couldn't believe what I was hearing. I was twenty years old and being physically threatened by my manager over a game of football! I had my mum and dad at the game, and now this? I took my gear off and went into the shower. Walter Smith had managed to calm the situation down a bit and came in to tell me I was going back out. I'm not ashamed to admit I was in tears. This all happened in the space of ten minutes, it was intense. I just thought, 'What the fuck is all this?'

Within ten minutes of the restart I'd put us 1-0 up. Luggy then scored an absolute beauty, right in the top corner but Holty was rather dubiously ruled offside. I said to him, 'What the hell are you doing that far up the park? You'll get a nose-bleed wandering away up there.' Rangers then went and punished us with two goals and the cup was lost. I just had to try and wipe the half-time episode from my mind and get on with it. It certainly wasn't the first major outburst and most definitely would not be the last.

There was no time for dwelling on the negative for the next morning we had to meet at Tannadice and ready ourselves for our UEFA Cup away tie with Winterslag of Belgium. One player was already in the dressing room when Richard Gough and I walked in. He was reading a newspaper which was held high covering his face. I strolled across and pulled it down revealing a very hung-over team mate. He'd been drinking pints and vodkas in a miners club in Fife and was suffering really badly. I told him he'd better stay well clear of the wee man or he'd get slaughtered.

The plane had barely taken off when the same player pressed the service button and asked the hostess for water, and lots of it. I can't remember if he spewed on the flight but when we got to our hotel he was spewing all over the place. The club doctor had to step in and administer a jag to stop the vomiting. Wee Jim arrived on the scene and asked the doctor what was happening but, give him his due, he told the manager our team mate had some sort of virus. He could have dropped him right in it but, instead, instructed him to rest with nil by mouth. When his hangover wore off it was hilarious because by then he was starving so a few of us had to go and fetch grub to sneak into his room.

On the night of the match the pitch was extremely wet and they wouldn't let us warm up on it but they did, however, let a marching band strut up and down the middle of it before we kicked off, turning it into a churned-up quagmire. We got a 0-0 draw but, really, their team weren't up to much and we gave them five in the return.

After the away tie Wee Jim allowed us to go out for a few

beers with the strict instructions 'don't overdo it'. Wattie was with us anyway so there's no way it was going to get out of hand, although he didn't mind a beer or two himself. We found an ideal place not far up the road, a truckers bar which had a pool table, so we set in about the beer and were having a great time. One of the players got chatting to a trucker who had this huge car-transporter lorry parked outside. Next thing we knew, he'd got the keys from the guy and went out into the cab. Another player (famed for his ability to lose the plot after three pints) climbed up onto the roof of the cab and was banging on the window. The cab then started up and drove off with the 'stuntman' terrified and hanging on for dear life!

Our newly trained trucker team mate drove it down the road to the hotel car park and pulled it up, only for Wee Jim to look out of his window and see one of his players driving a lorry and another hanging off the cab. I'm not sure what the outcome of that episode was (no doubt Wee Jim going crazy – especially after letting us out for a quiet pint!) but the lorry was returned to a very worried trucker who probably thought he'd seen the last of it and was now on its way to Germany!

There were of course occasions when boyish shenanigans crept into the dressing room, even when the mood was volatile. I had this daft trick inspired by Stan Laurel where I would fold my ears in on themselves then put my finger in my mouth and blow, which in turn made my ears pop back out. This was always a great party piece, especially when somebody else was getting a full round of the 'McLean guns'. There they were on the other side of the room being subjected to one of the most extreme forms of tongue-lashing that any manager could administer when bingo, they'd look up just in time to catch my ears popping out. The result was hilarious to watch as they struggled desperately not to smirk, or, worse still, burst out laughing in our irate gaffer's face. He did have his 'favourites' though, the ones who didn't get it so bad.

It wasn't so funny when the tables were turned and you were the one on the receiving end, and believe me I was! When you made a clanger during a game or were just having a bad 'forty-five' in general, that tunnel seemed as welcoming as a toxic fart in a sleeping bag. During the walk to the dressing room you were praying that some stupid arse would open their mouth and take the heat off you. The best policy was to sit quiet and just accept his wrath.

I remember one game at Tannadice when he was giving us his team talk before the match. He said, 'You'll need to watch out for this keeper 'cause he kicks a huge ball.' Davie Narey was sat right behind him gesturing with his arms and making the shape of a 'huge ball'. Everyone just crumbled, struggling hard not to explode in fits of laughter. You were, of course, walking a suicidal tightrope but moments like these were priceless. Wee Jim was always on his toes though and when I'd been out drinking on nights before training he was, understandably, looking to catch me out and reprimand me.

My dressing room peg was positioned right next to the door for the physio's room and he would deliberately walk in and out of there three or four times before declaring, 'This dressing room's reeking of drink!' It was his way of saying, 'I know someone's been on it,' but it could have been any one of us and he couldn't prove it. If I had been on the lash I tried to keep out of his way but sometimes when we were travelling to training in the minibus he'd manoeuvre the bodies so that I would have to go in the car with him. I'd have the window down having swilled mouthwash around for an hour earlier, be chewing on gum and generally trying not to breathe in his direction. He wasn't daft though and surely must have known I'd indulged in a few aperitifs.

Mind you, I wasn't the only player who enjoyed a drink at United, although I do admit I maybe enjoyed it a little more than the rest. A certain team mate had been out on a Thursday night with a few pals having a rare old time at Fat Sam's nightclub in Dundee. They were having a right carry-on when he jumped up and hit his head on an overhead stairway. Blood started to pour from the wound and he had to go to the hospital immediately to have it tended to. Next morning he turned up at the ground with this big blood-stained 'turban' on looking like shit. Wee Jim pulled him in and asked what had happened. 'Well,' he said, 'I woke up during the night and had to get up but I didn't see the dog on the floor and I tripped over it.' I said to him later, 'How the hell did you manage to get away with that when I get fined for the least little thing?' He just laughed, was cleaned up and was playing on the Saturday. I still don't know if he even owned a dog!

As I was positioned mostly on the right wing, some matches could be hellish when things weren't going to plan. If you were attacking the goal at the opposite end of the Shed it meant you were well within earshot for some of the manager's colourfully constructive 'advice'. Playing the second half was a joy although the tirade did still carry on albeit at a few decibels lower. Bannon, who often played on the opposite wing, used to take the piss out of him and would blatantly motion to his ears saying, 'What? I can't hear you. What are you saying?' Of course he knew damn well what McLean was saying – *the whole of the terrace knew what he was saying!*

Around about this time I had moved out of the family home in Douglas and into a house in nearby Broughty Ferry. What I didn't realise was that this simple event was going to cause a rather embarrassing situation for me. The embarrassment however would soon turn to anger. I had noticed a rash forming on my stomach which quickly spread to my upper torso so I went to the club doctor and asked him to take a look. After a brief examination he said, 'I think it's scabies.'

'What are you on about?' I replied. His next statement nearly floored me.

'Has your mum been washing your clothes or has she changed the powder she uses or something?'

I thought, 'You cheeky c***!' I went home and told my mum and she went mad. Never one for swearing she put her religious beliefs to one side and let rip full pelt at this damning accusation. She was furious that he could even suggest that she wasn't washing my clothes.

He gave me this cream for scabies which I applied for about three weeks but it was hopeless and the rash was getting worse. It then dawned on me that they (the club) didn't want to pay for me to be seen by a specialist. If it had been Davie Narey or some of the others they would have been up getting checked and back out without delay. Eventually they sent me up to Fernbrae Hospital where I was examined properly. When I pulled my shirt up the doctor said straight away, 'I know what that is – it's nerves.'

'What do you mean *nerves*?'

He continued, 'Well, at your stage in life you shouldn't really be nervous about anything.'

'I'm not,' I replied.

'Have you done anything different in your life recently?'

'Not that I can think of.' I paused for a moment then said, 'I've just bought a house but I . . .'

He cut in and said, 'That's what it is. It's something in your subconscious.' He gave me a five-day course of tablets to take. What he didn't tell me was not to take alcohol with them. Later on I went down to the St James' Club to watch the legendary Dundee band St Andrew and the Woollen Mill. I had a couple of pints and began to feel like my legs were made of rubber. After four I disintegrated into a heap on the floor. It was mental. I felt like I was in a trance and I wasn't in charge of my own body. Within five days the condition had gone. It angered me that the club could let one of their top players endure a lot of unnecessary discomfort which could have been dealt with far more efficiently.

After moving house I always popped back in to see my parents and made sure they were all right. More often than not my dad was in the kitchen – that was *his* room. He wouldn't let mum in there, he did all the cooking for us simply because he enjoyed it. I think it was also his space where he could sip whisky from his quarter bottle which he always kept with him. Anyway, I entered the house this particular afternoon and heard him moving about so I went down onto my hands and knees and quietly crawled through. His back was facing me so I grabbed the back of his calf and barked like a rabid dog. He nearly shat himself and put his knee right through the washing machine glass! Water poured out everywhere as the air filled with expletives.

'Ya stupid bastard, ya better get this cleaned up afore yir mither gets back!' he shouted. I couldn't believe what had happened and kept apologising but we all laughed about it later – much later!

My Old Man was always up for a wee laugh and I must admit there were times when I wound him up something awful. Mum used to give him something like £3 which was enough to get him his quarter bottle and three ten pence doubles and a ten pence treble at the bookies. It was during the close-season and I was sitting with my brother Keith and dad watching *Grandstand*. My Old Man asked if I'd nip up to the bookies and put his bets on for him. I came back later and he asked how his lines had done. I said, 'You're a jammy bastard aren't you, 33s, 20s and 16s?' and threw down over two hundred quid to him. He was all flummoxed; he'd never seen so much money in his life. He began divvying it up, 'Right, there's twenty to you Keith. Ralph, here's a tenner 'cause you've got loads of money. Give that to your mum and I'll keep the rest.'

I waited a moment then gathered all the money back up and said, 'Fuck off you daft arse, it's *my* money! You couldn't pick your nose!' He was going mental when he realised he'd been duped. 'What am I gonna do for a drink now?' he shouted. I asked Keith to go up to the shop and get a case of lager and a quarter bottle of whisky but told him to bring it to me first. When he returned I got the empty bottle and filled it with cold tea, poured a large nip and took it through to him in the living room. 'Have you calmed down now?' I asked then gave him the glass. He put it straight down in a oner then screwed his face up.

'What the hell is *that* pish? Is it Japanese whisky or something?' I came clean and told him it was cold tea. He went off his head again before I gave him the bottle. He took it in great spirits though and we would always have a crack like that.

In the March of that season we came up against Radnicki Nis of Yugoslavia in the quarter-finals of the UEFA Cup. After going 2-0 up at Tannadice we travelled away for the second leg fairly confident that we could reach the semi-finals. It was a poor country and, as the ground had no floodlights, the match had to be played in the afternoon. The vast majority of spectators were military personnel all decked out in their army uniforms and the atmosphere was very hostile. We had to endure bouts of spitting and coin-throwing. The match itself turned out to be one of the biggest cons ever. The referee only lived about sixty miles away in the old East Germany and he was giving all sorts to them. We went behind 2-0 and were really up against it. As the game moved into the latter stages the ref produced an unbelievable decision from nothing and awarded them a penalty. Hamish had come out to meet a high ball in the box and punched it clear. One of their players barged into him and the ref awarded the spot-kick. We lost 3-2 on aggregate and went crashing out of the competition. It was a miserable feeling. Try telling me there's no money changing hands in the game. In my opinion I reckon the ref could have probably bought a house out of what he got from that – albeit in East Germany!

We finished the season fourth in the League and empty-handed. The only consolation was we'd be competing in the UEFA Cup once more. Still, the signs were encouraging and we had the nucleus of a very good side, most of which had been together now for some time. For all Wee Jim's rantings and occasionally flying off the handle like a maniac with a bag of wasps in his Y-Fronts, he had built a formidable outfit capable of taking on anyone on their day. I had played in most of the games and returned a decent haul of goals from the wing. There was, however, always room for improvement and the next season would be a case of 'go again' and see what happens.

5

THE TANGERINE MACHINE
GOES ROLLING!

Following the usual regime of torturous pre-season fitness work we went on a Scandinavian tour which began with a match in Sweden against Malmo where we were soundly beaten 3-1. We then moved on to Denmark for a few matches and it was during one of these that there was a bizarre occurrence which had Wee Jim going absolutely apeshit. It seems laughable now but back then (in Britain anyway) we still had ballboys chasing the match ball when it went out of play. This Danish team we were playing were well ahead of the game though, and (unknown to us at the time) had spare balls for their ballboys to lob back on to keep play flowing whenever the ball went out of play – something we now take for granted. Anyway, the ball went out of play and naturally we were all expecting the original ball to be retrieved before play continued. I think Wee Jim was still looking for it when they lobbed the spare on, went up the park and crashed it into the net, much to our bewilderment. When he realised what had happened he went completely off his rocker!

We had a right laugh though when Goughie and I got hold

of the key to John Gardiner and Hamish McAlpine's room. We filled the bath up and lobbed all John's clothes into it. We left Hamish's, however, for fear of a smack in the jaw! Wee Jim called a team meeting at 4pm to discuss tactics for the match that night. Any events like these you were expected to promptly turn up wearing the club tracksuit. The squad were already in when John turned up about ten seconds late wearing a pair of flip-flops, shorts and a T-shirt. Wee Jim looked at him in disbelief thinking he was taking the piss or something. Big John tried to explain that his room had been trashed and that all his gear was wet but the gaffer was having none of it and fined him. I thought, 'Shit, we've gone too far this time!' He never did find out it was us.

As was the norm, the League Cup competition kick-started the season in earnest and we produced an early run of victories before the League curtain raiser against our fellow east coast neighbours, Aberdeen. They had a very good side at the time and were in contention for the League Championship most seasons, actually winning it in 79/80. Together, both teams had been enough of a thorn in the Old Firm's side for someone to label us the 'New Firm'. Celtic also had a fantastic side during that era whilst Rangers were performing below the high levels which they and their fans expected and demanded.

Our growing European pedigree and ability, especially at grabbing results on foreign turf, was probably one of the major factors in determining what happened in season 82/83. For me it all began that night when we won in Monaco back in September 1981. The psychological effects of that result planted the seeds of self-belief necessary to build on and hopefully achieve greater things.

As we sat in the Tannadice dressing room awaiting that first match to get underway, at no point did any of the players or the manager say, 'This might just be our year.' There was never much talk from us anyway in there, we simply listened to the gaffer's team talk then went about our business in the hope of securing the two points. This we did with a 2-0 win and the campaign was off and running.

Our League form gathered momentum and with it, progression in the UEFA Cup too. Again, away results, firstly in Holland against PSV Eindhoven and then over in Norway against Viking Stavanger, proved decisive. Three days after our home tie with the Norwegians we travelled north for a League tussle with our New Firm sparring partners Aberdeen at Pittodrie. Having already beaten them three times that season, including home and away victories in the League Cup, our mood was positive. We'd have been as well making sandcastles on the Aberdeen beach though as the Dons thumped us 5-1. Celtic added to our misery four days later when they knocked us out of the League Cup in a close semi-final encounter.

I remember being involved in an entirely different occasion from football up at Pittodrie when one of their players was having his testimonial game. A half-time penalty box to penalty box race was organised between one player from each of the twelve clubs with the sponsors putting up £300 for the winner, £150 for second and £50 for third. Wee Jim had put me forward as Dundee United's representative but I didn't want to go. In the end I had to and travelled up with Richard Gough. We were all sitting in the dressing room before the event and I said to John Halpin from Celtic, 'What are you going to do with the dough if you win John?'

'I've just bought a new car and that'll pay for the insurance,' he replied. I didn't say anything but I knew he wasn't going to win. I was sure the guy representing Dundee FC was a goalkeeper and an ex-Powderhall sprinter so I knew I was in for some stiff competition. We all went out onto the park and the starter gun wouldn't work so the guy said he'd blow a whistle instead but he blew it twice and half went and half didn't. I was one of those who never ran and I watched as John Halpin raced over the line first and was giving it loads. Unfortunately for him they decided to re-run it, which was comical.

I realised this was it and I'd have to get a sharp start, so when he blew I took off. I hit the front and knew I had the beating of the Dundee goalie, who was next to me. As we approached the finish line I thought, 'This is a doddle, it's in the bag,' and I took the foot off the gas. Next thing, the guy from Partick Thistle waltzed past me and won the race. I couldn't believe it! I was gutted. Back at Tannadice Wee Jim ripped into me for letting the club down and finishing second. He wasn't even there to see it.

I was involved in a similar event for another testimonial match at Arbroath a year or two later. Again, I couldn't be bothered with it, having played the day before; I just wanted to enjoy my rest day. I went down with Stuart Beedie and I was coasting to the finish line when my hamstring went. I was still far enough ahead to win the race easy. Afterwards, Stuart and I went on the piss, but rather than report the injury on the Monday morning, I had the day off so I went in on the Tuesday and told Andy Dickson I'd pulled it whilst swimming when I kicked off from the side of the pool. If I'd said what the real cause of it was Wee Jim would've got to hear about it, gone bananas and blamed me for not warming up properly, so the swimming did the trick and nobody was any the wiser.

The 82/83 season was to have some major turning points and one of those came the following Saturday when we entertained Rangers at Tannadice. I scored to put us 1-0 up then, midway through the second half, we found ourselves 2-1 down. We were all over them. Doddsy grabbed an equaliser and with about four minutes remaining Richard Gough put us into the lead with a great goal. He took one touch then blasted a terrific 'daisy-cutter' along the deck which cracked in off the post. There must only have been about a minute left on the clock when Rangers took the kick-off and incredibly gave the ball straight back to us. Luggy played me away into the far corner with their defence screaming for offside. There was no way I was offside, I was gone, left them all for dead. I had plenty of time to turn and look about, expecting everyone to be up with me but there was no one. Their goalie came out to block me but I already knew what I was going to do. I hit it with the outside of my right boot and watched as it rattled in the top corner. I remember turning around to Wee Jim and saying, 'What about that then?' It was one of my favourite goals ever.

We had another couple of great results home and away against the German side Werder Bremen in the UEFA Cup which put us through to the quarter-finals. It was early March 1983 when we faced our opponents Bohemians of Prague in the first leg in Czechoslovakia. We played well in that match but ultimately returned home with a 1-0 defeat. Still, we were confident in our ability to overturn that result. In the League we had managed to keep in touch with Aberdeen and Celtic, constantly snapping at both their heels. The Saturday before the second leg of our UEFA Cup tie we faced our old adversaries and city neighbours Dundee at Tannadice. We didn't realise it at the time but this match and its outcome proved hugely significant in the story which was unfolding. Our initial two goal lead was cancelled out with three strikes from Dundee before we pulled our socks up and eventually ran out 5-3 winners.

Four days later we took to the field at Tannadice for our second leg tie with Bohemians hoping to mark another monumental occasion in the team's history and give the fans a glory night to remember. Sadly, it wasn't to be. We pummelled them relentlessly but just couldn't find the breakthrough. I'm sure one goal that night would have turned into a deluge. At the end of the ninety we were left only with the thoughts of what might have been.

The following few days were sorely depressing. Everyone was on a complete downer. We were now out of all cup competitions (St Mirren had mugged us in the Scottish Cup before we even got started). The League was a long shot but at least we were still in with a shout. Wee Jim believed we had as good a chance as Aberdeen or Celtic although we trailed them in third place by a few points. Aberdeen, our next opponents, were in pole position and their morale was sky-high following their European Cup Winners' Cup heroics when they defeated Bayern Munich. They'd succeeded in reaching a Euro semi where we had failed and they quite rightly must have felt we were there for the taking. (On 11 May Alex Ferguson steered his team to Euro glory in Gothenburg with an incredible display beating Real Madrid 2-1 in the final after extra time.) The gaffer had other ideas however and told the press if we could win at Pittodrie on the Saturday then we were right back in it. The problem was how do we lift the gloom and fire ourselves up again?

Match day came and Luggy was injured (as usual!) so Jim approached me and said, 'I want you to play up front against Alex McLeish and Willie Miller, you'll be too quick for them.' As we travelled north on the team bus I remember thinking, 'I'm not looking forward to this.' I just had a bad feeling. Anyway, we got up there and went out onto the pitch for the warm-up and I had a change of mindset. I said to myself, 'Ach fuck it, let's get on with this and see what we can get out of it.'

We started well and had Aberdeen on the rack. They were unprepared for our aggressive onslaught which put them on the back foot. When Richard Gough went charging down the right I found myself square to him and I'm shouting, 'Richy, Richy, give's the ball!' He passed it; I took one touch then struck it with my left foot. It went in off the bar and bounced out. Their keeper Jim Leighton's screaming, 'It wasn't in! It wasn't in!' It was over by a mile – goal! We're up 1-0 and the mood changed to 'hey, something might happen here.'

Next thing, Derek Stark gets to the byline on the left wing. Now when did anyone ever see Starky away up there? He put in a cross and I'm sure it was Willie Miller who made a complete arse of it and let the ball roll to my feet. I slotted it in off the post and we're up 2-0 and dominating the match. We should have had them buried. Of course they were getting angry by now and were well wound up. We went in at half-time and the Wee Man was delighted. In the second half wee Strach (Gordon Strachan) scored a penalty for them and the tension really mounted. I had been giving McLeish a hard time the whole game and he was not a happy man. I was never one for giving 'verbal' to my opposite numbers but they'd try it on, attempting to wind me up. I much preferred to kick the ball past them and take off.

They had a corner which broke out to me and I found myself one-on-one with Big Alex in the centre circle. I decided to see what he had in the tank and flicked it past him. He deliberately ran straight into me then ended up on the deck. I was so angry after all the previous fouling I swung my boot at him and just missed his head. I'm just so thankful I did miss him because it was full-on! Then he lay there *holding his balls!* I told the referee he was a wanker and just walked off. It was a crazy thing to do and all credit to the lads as they held on magnificently for the 2-1 victory.

As you can imagine, the stakes were high for this match, a win would keep us in contention for the League and I think we had been promised a bonus payment of £500. This was way in excess of the normal £300. At the end of the game I was already suited and sitting in the dressing room waiting on the Hoover when in he (McLean) came. He went absolutely mental! 'You fuckin' wee bastard, you put all the rest of your mates under pressure [blah, blah, blah]!' Of course I couldn't say anything. If I did he would have just exploded all the more. His final words were, 'I'm not even going to fine you a week's wages this week.' I was like, 'Thank God for that!' (My wage at the time was only about £220). He continued, 'I'm just not giving you the bonus!' Sure, the match could've ended a whole lot differently due to my recklessness but the bottom line was I'd kept us in the running for the League and was denied a single penny from the bonus. I ended up with about £140 in wages. I think I drank it all in one night!

The way results were going it was like being on a roller coaster without a seat belt. One week Aberdeen had the upper hand, then it would be Celtic's turn, then we'd pitch in only to have our good work undone by some below-par performance. From now on in, every game was a must-win if we wanted to have any chance of winning the League. I remember the two trips to Parkhead in particular. These matches were rearranged fixtures against Celtic, both midweek and only a fortnight apart. The first one ended in defeat and dropped us back down the pecking order. This may sound daft but I remember we were at the Airdrie roundabout and the Spandau Ballet hit 'True' was on the radio. Two weeks later we travelled back through and guess what was playing at the Airdrie roundabout – 'True'! I thought, 'Déjà vu? Nah I'm not having this.'

We were in the driving seat and leading 2-1 when Richy Gough saw red and was sent packing. The inevitable onslaught followed which we bravely managed to withstand for a period. Then the roof caved in and they equalised. It was backs-against-the-wall stuff as they went for the killer blow but to a man we yielded nothing. It was now or never. With only a few minutes remaining Eamonn Bannon tore down the wing, cut back onto his right then crossed it. I got in front of their defender Mark Reid, took it on my chest and hit a left foot volley right over keeper Packie Bonner and straight into the net! The whole place went silent, apart that is, from our travelling Arab band. I ran away to celebrate, waiting on the players to come up – and got cramp! I was like, 'Aw ya bastard!' I had to limp through those last few minutes, but it was well worth it! We were only a point off the top now.

I was in the Fort Bar in Broughty Ferry later with Richard

Gough having a couple of beers. Walter Smith was there and I'm sure Gordon Wallace was also there. It wasn't a session, far from it. Walter would never have allowed that. Anyway we were having a conversation and he said to me, 'Do you think we'll win it (the League) Ralph?' I don't know if my reply was just bravado or what but I laughed and said, 'Win it? Look who we have left to play!' He looked at me as if questioning my sanity.

On the Saturday we gave Killie a bit of a doing and put four past them and in doing so went top of the League thanks to a 1-0 win by Aberdeen who beat Celtic at Pittodrie. The following week we had to travel away to Greenock and Morton's ground Cappielow. Nobody liked going to Morton, it was a horrible place. We had a huge travelling support go through with us which was subsidised by the club. Wee Jim was that dighted (absent-minded) he forgot that it was free buses only and thought everyone was getting into the ground for free as well. He actually gave the same team talk to us twice in the dressing room. I sat there looking at the rest and thinking, 'Has anybody else clocked this?' I was told later he had been given tablets to calm him down.

During the match Hamish got injured and Heggie had to go in the goal. Graeme Payne (who was out on loan at the time) was playing for them that day. He'd already played in a couple of matches for us earlier in the season. There was one comical incident in the game when I was about to take a corner and here's one of my very good friends being arrested and marched past me by the local constabulary. I laughed and said to him, 'Where are *you* going?'

The result was never in any doubt though and big Davie (Narey) and Doddsy both notched. Holty played me through against their central defender big Joe McLaughlin. Joe was quick but he dived in and I strode past him and rolled it under their keeper. The game finished 4-0 and the tangerine machine kept rolling. Our penultimate match was against Motherwell at Tannadice and they were also dealt with mercilessly and hammered 4-0. Our fate was now in our own hands.

6

DESTINY AT DENS

The scene was set for the final chapter of a story which began the previous year at Tannadice on 4 September 1982. Not even the greatest of literary geniuses could have scripted a plot as twisted and darkly beautiful as the one set to kick off on 14 May at 3.00pm, Dens Park, Dundee. In order to make club history and satisfy the tangerine half of the city, we would have to beat our great rivals from across the street in the most important derby ever! The fact we had beaten them three times already during the season mattered not. In derby matches throughout the world form goes out the proverbial window when that first whistle blows and battle commences. The two other challengers for the title, Celtic and Aberdeen, had ties against Rangers and Hibs respectively, but it was of no concern to us. We knew what *we* had to do.

Earlier in the season we had gone through to Glasgow on a shopping trip where we headed for Ralph Slater's to buy new suits. Luggy had a friend who owned a jeweller's and some of us went there and bought bits and pieces. On the morning of the match I put my new suit on and phoned all my family and told them they had to come to this game. Quite often I used to say to my dad before games, 'Dad, I'll score today.' On the phone I said those exact same words that morning. He never used to say a lot, he'd just keep quiet and let me get on with it. He didn't go to too many games either. He preferred to watch the highlights on TV in the comfort of his living room.

There were no fancy preparations for the match, it was all very laid back and relaxed (on the surface anyway!). I don't think we even went for a pre-match meal. I parked my car down at the Radio Tay buildings in North Isla Street and walked up to Dens from there. It was very surreal. I was walking up the road with my fiancée Kim and we just mixed in with the fans on the way. They were all asking, 'Ralph, do you think we'll win today?'

'Ach, they're only a pub team. We'll win no bother!' It was all just banter and bravado though and there was certainly no disrespect meant to Dundee Football Club. In the dressing room Wee Jim gave his team talk, nothing extravagant, it just went along the lines of his usual spiel. We all knew what was at stake and what was required. It's fair to say, he was a bag of nerves. An article appeared in one of the papers afterwards which quoted something like, 'We were all nervous apart from Ralph – he's not got a nerve in his body!' I laughed and thought, 'You cheeky bastard, I've got feelings as well you know.'

It was kind of strange in a way, we as a team hardly exchanged a word between ourselves. I don't know about the rest of the lads but my own thoughts were, 'We just *can't* let this go. We've come too far to let it slip.' The team which lined up that day were either about to be immortalised in

United folklore or would fade into the memories of those same punters as the 'nearly men'.

The team sheet read: McAlpine, Stark, Malpas, Gough, Hegarty, Narey, Bannon, Milne, Kirkwood, Sturrock and Dodds. Subs: Holt, Reilly.

The moment we left the dressing room and went out onto the park you could sense the enormity of the occasion. The fans were tremendous and gave us a massive lift. As the match kicked off the main thing going through each of our minds was to stay focused on the job in hand. I was playing on the right wing; Luggy wasn't injured for once and was up front with Doddsy. Whenever Luggy used to get the ball he would always look for Bannon or me. The first ball he played to me was way too far in front and their defender Stewart McKimmie passed it back easily to keeper Colin Kelly. I turned and said to him, 'Do you think I've got a fuckin' motorbike or something?' (My Suzuki was long gone by then!)

The next one he slipped on his arse as he passed it through the middle. This time I cut in from the right across McKimmie and collected it thinking I could maybe get up the inside of him. He dived in so I flicked the ball through his legs and the whole thing just opened up. Kirky committed a cardinal sin when he ran across me, something you're drilled never to do. Thankfully it didn't distract me and I advanced on the Dundee defence who kept backing off. Everything just flashed through my mind – pass it to Doddsy on the left whose left foot wasn't his strongest asset. Kirky on the right was out of the question – he would have hoofed it into the TC Keay end! In a split second I looked up and saw Kelly off his line and thought, 'I've got him here, if I can just pull it off.' From about twenty-five yards out I chipped it with my left and watched as the ball sailed inch-perfect over his stretching hand and into the net. The tangerine and black legions erupted.

I turned and cheered towards the TV camera then focused on my dad up in the stand and gestured to him with 'I did it dad!' It was the proudest moment of my life and I'm sure, the proudest moment in my dad's life. Having celebrated my twenty-second birthday the previous day, this was the best present I could ever have wished for. There was only four minutes on the clock. We still had a hell of a long way to go.

Shortly afterwards we were awarded a penalty when big Davie (Narey) was dropped in the box. How Eamonn (Bannon) was allowed to take the penalty I'll never know. He was our regular taker but I felt I should have been given the job as my confidence was sky-high. The ref blew for the kick to be taken and thankfully he stuck it away after Kelly had saved the first effort, but it was jittery stuff. The woodwork came to Dundee's rescue twice with efforts from Luggy and Doddsy and we should have been home and dry. Dundee then pulled a goal back and 'threw a cat amongst the pigeons' as they say. Iain Ferguson rifled in a shot and left Hamish with no chance. We went in 2-1 up at half-time and Wee Jim basically told us, 'more of the same' for what would be the most important forty-five minutes in the club's history. In terms of a footballing spectacle the second half was crap. Dundee did come more into it and gave us a couple of scares. I thought we might have been given a second penalty when I cut across Iain Macdonald and he fouled me, but the ref waved play on. I can only talk from a personal point of view when I say I didn't feel anxious or nervous but you could definitely feel the nail-biting tension in the air and sense the restlessness of our fans.

I remember Hamish shouting from his goal to the United fans packed in the TC Keay end behind him, 'What time is it? How long to go?' There was a great big bloody clock which nearly everyone in the ground could see, just over to his right! As the match entered its final moments I made my way down to the bottom end of the park and hung about near the tunnel waiting for the ref to blow. There was no way I was waiting for the stampede of our pitch-invading fans to engulf us! As the final whistle blew Cammy Fraser fired the ball at Richard Gough and tried to smack him on the head with it. Richy just gave it the 'up yours mate!' He didn't care. How could he? We were champions of Scotland! Just how tight it actually was in the end is illustrated in the final League placings below.

	P	W	D	L	F	A	Pts
1. Dundee United	36	24	8	4	90	35	56
2. Celtic	36	25	5	6	90	36	55
3. Aberdeen	36	25	5	6	76	24	55
4. Rangers	36	13	12	11	52	41	38
5. St Mirren	36	11	12	13	47	51	34
6. Dundee	36	9	11	16	42	53	29
7. Hibernian	36	7	15	14	35	51	29
8. Motherwell	36	11	5	20	39	73	27
9. Morton	36	6	8	22	30	74	20
10. Kilmarnock	36	3	11	22	28	91	17

It was hard to describe the feelings at the end of the game. I don't think it really sunk in till much later just what we had achieved. I don't even think it registered with Wee Jim till later either. There was a bizarre moment when he was walking down from the dugout shaking hands with our fans when one guy climbed onto the track and Wee Jim was trying to shove him back into the crowd. We'd just won the League and were thinking, 'What the hell are you worrying about that for?' It was genuinely great to see him smiling though when Gough and Heggie picked him up and hoisted him high onto their shoulders. I received the Man of the Match award which was a great honour. It was, and always will be, the proudest moment of my life. I finished the season with twenty-one goals in all competitions, which wasn't bad for a winger.

Back in the dressing room the champagne was popped and we were all congratulating each other. We had to go back out and salute the fans with a lap of honour. At first the authorities weren't going to allow it but eventually saw sense and we were able to enjoy the momentous occasion. More champagne followed in the team bath as press and TV people milled around and then we all went out to meet with our girlfriends and wives before walking back down the road to Tannadice. The boardroom was buzzing with activity as more interviews were conducted and we savoured the moment.

That night we were due to attend a United Supporters Association Player of the Year dance in Coupar Angus. The timing was unfortunate given the day's exceptional circumstances but these are the guys who pay their hard-earned money to stand in the terraces and support us and without them there would be no club. We had a duty to go, simple as that but, to be honest, on what was by far the biggest night of all our lives we just wanted to get out on the town and celebrate. We were allowed to have a drink but obviously had to remember we were representing the club and conduct ourselves accordingly.

It was 11 o'clock before we returned to Dundee. Me and Kim went back to Frank Kopel's house in Monifieth and didn't leave there till five in the morning. On that same Sunday morning everyone had to report in to Tannadice for 10.30am for a testimonial game in Forfar – kick-off time 12pm. This was organised as a pre-event for the celebrations which were taking place at the city's Chamber of Commerce at 4pm. Someone was definitely having a laugh but it certainly wasn't us!

We all sat there reeking of booze in a dressing room the size of a small phone box thinking, 'What the fuck are we doing here?' Just to add to the hilarity, the rain was lashing in horizontal. I'm not kidding, it was a total monsoon. No one really said anything; we were all just shaking our heads in disbelief. I elbowed Gough who was sat next to me and said, 'Watch this.'

'Ralph, don't,' he whispered.

I called out to Wee Jim, 'Hey Boss.'

'Aye,' he answered.

'See now that we've won the League?'

'Aye?'

'Any chance I can get all my fines back?'

'What do you mean?'

'Well, I've seen a house in the Ferry that I want to pay cash for!'

Of course everyone is sniggering by now. He didn't see the funny side of it and said, 'You're not funny ya wee c***!'

We went out to play the game (well, apart from Luggy because he was injured!) and everyone who played on the

Saturday started on the Sunday. One by one he replaced everybody with substitutions – except me! He made me play that whole ninety minutes.

It was still teeming with rain when we arrived back in Dundee for the civic reception and a tour in the open-top bus. Fair play to the punters who turned out in their thousands to cheer us on, it was fantastic. After we did all the official stuff and met with the Lord Provost, Kim and I headed back to the Ferry. That was it – I decided to go on a *proper* bender and celebrate big style!

That whole campaign, which had culminated in our historic League win, had some of the gloss taken from it when our manager made a controversial statement afterwards in the local paper and said, '. . . when you consider what they have achieved has been accomplished from a squad of only twelve players who have played consistently in the team.' I think there were twenty of us involved at some point or another throughout that season and every single one of us to a man contributed collectively in one way or another to achieve that Championship win. We were an incredibly tight-knit group who worked extremely well together. The most important factor of all was we were all mates. There were no egos or prima donnas, it just wouldn't have been allowed. Anybody trying that kind of nonsense would simply have been slaughtered from the rest so everyone just pulled as a team to help the cause and the result of that is now etched in the history books forever. It was a hugely disrespectful thing to say and some of the lads were rightfully bitter at hearing this. Guys like Iain Phillip, Ian Britton and even Graeme Payne among others had done their bit. Boney (John Reilly) had weighed in with seven goals and had every right to be pissed off. I think the whole nature of how vitally important each and every little contribution was, was demonstrated in Derek Murray's only appearance of the season when he saved a goal-bound shot off the line in a match against Motherwell. We eventually ran out 4-1 winners but it was little things like that, the last-gasp tackles, busting the balls to get back and cover and such that turned results in our favour. All of these things, together with the goals, saves, tactics, training and coaching went into making the whole jigsaw complete. That one reckless statement from Wee Jim left an unnecessary bad taste in the mouth for many of us.

7

THE BEAUTIFUL GAME?

Being crowned champions of Scotland brought with it the honour of representing our country in the best knockout club tournament in the world – the European Cup. Everyone connected with Dundee United was relishing the prospect of possible progress in that competition and the chance to go toe-to-toe with some of the footballing elite. This of course was the good old days when you had to *win* your respective league to play in the European Cup and not gain entry (like nowadays) through the back door.

There was however the small matter of defending the League title and the manager in his wisdom felt the need to strengthen the first team squad, not I may add with any big name signings. My own feelings on this were that it brought unnecessary disruption to a team which had been fluid and consistent. 'If it ain't broke don't fix it,' as the saying goes.

Pre-season we travelled to Spain for a mini tournament against RCD Espanyol and a Brazilian team called America de Rio. Argentinean legend Mario Kempes was playing for Espanyol but never broke so much as a bead of sweat. I think he was in dispute with his club Valencia and had been bumped so he wasn't interested. We won 2-0, which meant we would face the Brazilians in the final in Tarragona. We were getting beat at half-time and Wee Jim announced, 'No one's going out for the second half.' We didn't have a clue what was going on and the next thing we heard was the manager out in the corridor bawling and shouting. Our club hadn't been paid their share for taking part in the tournament so all hell broke loose. After an age spent sitting in the dressing room the matter was resolved and we went out for the second half. We lost 2-1 to a very good side. They had a little left-winger who was absolutely tremendous. Gough and I spent most of our time trying to catch him.

We then had two friendly matches at Tannadice against top English opposition, the first being West Ham, whom we walloped 4-0. I scored with a cracking chip from inside the box, which was quite a feat considering their keeper Phil Parkes was a big man. I'd scored against him some six months previously in February when we went down to Upton Park and drew 2-2. The night before that match Wee Jim made me play in the reserves against Cowdenbeath and I remember it was absolutely freezing. This was great preparation for catching a flight down to London at the crack of dawn the next morning! We flew straight home after that for someone's dinner in The Ballinard Hotel in the Ferry and grabbed a well-deserved pint. We actually played West Ham quite a few times in friendlies, which I'm sure was down to former United man Ray Stewart signing for them in 1979 and the clubs kept up a healthy relationship. The next game was against Spurs for Hamish The Goalie's testimonial, which finished all square at 1-1.

Following those two matches we kicked off the season

proper, but there was no euphoric feeling of getting the campaign underway. To be honest I felt a bit dispirited and this was down to Wee Jim whom I felt was moving the goal-posts and shuffling things round too much with team selections, but he *was* the manager I suppose.

At the end of September Dundee United travelled away to Malta to face Hamrun Spartans in the club's historical first ever match in the European Cup. Rangers had also drawn Maltese opposition Valletta and were due to play in the same stadium on the same pitch just hours before we were. As United were a lot less well off than Rangers, our club asked if they would like to share a chartered jet. The offer was declined. We had to travel to Edinburgh for a scheduled flight to Heathrow, then on to Malta, and who was on the same flight? *Glasgow Rangers!*

We knew our opponents weren't up to much but still gave them their due respect. We went in 2-0 up at the break and for the second half myself and Gough were on the far side, away from the dugout and the wee man's rantings. At full time we had secured a comfortable 3-0 away win but the manager was not amused. He shouted to me, 'What were you and Gough up to that second half?'

'What do you mean?' I asked.

'You two could've put your fuckin' suits on and they would have been *cleaner* when you came back in!'

That night we both had the usual foreign carry-on and turned Bannon and Kirkwood's room upside down putting the mattresses in the bath, emptying the toothpaste out and spreading polish about etc. We were always at it. Born in Sweden, I remember when Richy (Gough) first came to the club from South Africa, around about the time I was breaking into the first team. His Old Man Charlie was Scottish and had played professionally for Charlton. He wanted his son to play for Rangers and quite coincidentally an ex-player or scout was out there and noticed Richard. I'm sure he was due to be conscripted into their army at the time and so he upped and left for Scotland and a trial with Rangers. They already had enough central defenders and he was turned away after his trial but this worked out very favourably for Dundee United when he signed shortly afterwards.

His first match was for the reserves down at Arbroath and I turned up to watch him. It was also to show Wee Jim that I wasn't in the boozer. Richy was playing everything with the outside of his boot and I was thinking to myself, 'He's (McLean) gonna hate that!' His philosophy was, if you played like that you didn't have enough ball control. I didn't think Wee Jim would entertain him but history shows what a great player he became for United. This was the Tuesday so when Friday came I said to him, 'Richard, what are you doing at the weekend?'

'Nothing,' he replied.

'Do you fancy coming out for a beer after the game?'

'Yeah, that would be great Ralph.'

We went down to the Ferry and I met up with a few of the lads then we headed on to The Sands nightclub with a pocket full of free passes. It was very noisy inside as you can imagine and I asked Richy what he wanted to drink.

'I'll have a *Becks* please c***!' I ordered up two bottles. A little later I said, 'It's your round Richy.'

'What? Do we have to pay?' he asked.

'Of course you have to pay, what do you think this is?'

It came back to my round again and I asked him if he wanted another beer. 'Yes, I'll have another *Becks* please c***.'

'Right, wait a minute. Hold it right there! See the first time, I thought I misheard you. Don't speak to me like that ever again. I've brought you out here to mix with the lads and see a bit of the city, and you're calling me a *c****?

'Sorry Ralph sorry, it's just that's the way they speak in South Africa!'

'Well this is Broughty-fuckin'-Ferry, not South Africa so don't speak to me like that again!' After that we were best of mates.

One of our bevvy sessions landed us in hot water after a certain player (whom we'll call 'The Car Cleaner') shopped us to Wee Jim. He was paid back in kind though when I found out. We were playing Motherwell at Tannadice and went in at half-time 2-0 up. Wee Jim was doing his usual ranting so I quietly said to Richy, 'Toilet'.

'What's up?' he asked.

'See when you get the ball this half, fire it at the Car Cleaner and keep doing it, don't pass to me. When I get the ball I'll do the same, just keep feeding him it. His first touch is shite.'

'What do you mean Ralph, I don't understand?'

'It was him who grassed on us last week!'

Five minutes into the second half the wee man's off the bench raging at him, 'You, ya useless bastard, you've got five fuckin' minutes and you're off!'

'Richy,' I said, 'keep it going,' and so we just kept pinging it at him and eventually succeeded in getting him the 'big hook'. In the showers afterwards he came up to us and said, 'Thanks for that boys.'

'Thanks for what?' I said. 'Are you talking to me?'

'You know what you did out there.'

'It's not my fault you've got a crap first touch and anyway, you're better sticking to cleaning the wee man's car. If you grass on us again I'll wipe you out!' Gough didn't know where to look.

The second leg of the Hamrun Spartans tie was a mere formality and I notched a brace in a repeat of the first game, giving us a comfortable 6-0 aggregate scoreline.

In the mid-October of 1983, and on the back of some very good form, we travelled away to Belgium for the next round of the European Cup and a crack at our old sparring partners Standard Liege. Five years previously they had knocked us out of the UEFA Cup, so we had a little score to settle. We played particularly well on the night and came away with a very positive 0-0 draw. With confidence running high, we were sure we could take them at Tannadice and progress to the quarter-finals.

That second leg tie is one which will stay clear in my memory forever and I don't mind admitting it's probably one of the best games I've ever played in. I managed to grab two of the goals in a stylish and totally commanding 4-0 victory. That night, Dundee United were on fire and the team performance was one of near flawless perfection. Luggy paid me a massive compliment after the match when he said, 'That wasn't Dundee United versus Standard Liege, that was *Ralph Milne* versus Standard Liege. He ran the show!' We had just booked ourselves a place in the quarter-finals with a thoroughly convincing and merciless performance.

In manager Jim McLean's book *Jousting With Giants* he described with great honesty and passion his unharnessed delight and satisfaction at the team's performance over both those legs. He wrote:

Over the two ties against Standard Liege my players picked up the challenge better than they have ever done before or since. Over the two games, a fortnight apart as always, they produced the most perfect performance out of all the seventy or so ties we have ever played in Europe. Most of you will have realised by now, if you had not a fair idea before, that I am not the kind of manager who is given to singing the praises of his players too much. This time there was no other way I could describe the performances they produced over the 180 minutes of football. It was as if all the lessons they had learned in previous years, and all the teaching they had had from myself and the coaching staff, had reached fruition. As team displays go I cannot think of any to match them in all the years I've been with the club. For once I could sit back and enjoy some of the play, relax and savour the achievements of the club, because out there in front of us was the realisation of hours and days and years of training and talking, of listening and learning, of practising and preparing, of working and waiting.

The waiting was made worthwhile in Belgium and then again at Tannadice in the return. Over the two games we defeated the Belgian side tactically. We defeated them individually. We defeated them by playing the Continental game better than they were able to do themselves. Over there we controlled the tie. It went the way we wanted it to go. It took the pattern we imposed on the match. Rarely, if at all, did we look in any danger of defeat.

Then came the return and the worry leading up to that game that perhaps our form could not be sustained for the second leg. That was soon washed away as we again established control and in another superb performance we were able to win 4-0 in front of a crowd of 18,500.

71

These were of course magnificent words from a man who was so hard to please and who constantly sought perfection from his players and his teams. My personal joy soon turned to pain, however, and my emotions plunged from blissful ecstasy to numbing heartache. The then Scotland manager Jock Stein had witnessed our Tannadice demolition job of the Belgian champions and I was very confident of at least being selected for the next squad. Coincidentally, the week previous to the first leg I had played for the Under-21s against Belgium and hoped the call would come for the bigger stage. As it turned out, I was named as one of the over-age players again in the Under-21 squad and, with that single action, my dream of playing for my country at full international level died. From that moment I knew I would never gain a Scottish cap. How could I? No one gets named as an over-age player in an Under-21 squad at the age of twenty-two! Back then, when over-age players were included in the squad, they were usually older men who could offer the young guys a wealth of experience and leadership. In my opinion I believe Jock Stein was 'advised' that this was the better option by my own manager Jim McLean and here I was now bearing the fruits of that volatile relationship.

During season 81/82 I came on as a sub against Sweden in an Under-21s match, but at that time I was quite happy to be at that level and just be included in the set up. But when you get to this level (playing in European Cups) and are performing to the highest standards then I feel I merited a shout for a full cap, no two ways about it. When you put your lot in and don't get your just rewards then you are inclined to feel slightly pissed off. Although some of our players had been selected for Scotland there did still exist the feeling of a

West Coast bias towards the Celtic and Rangers players, some-thing which many believe is still in evidence even nowadays. I would have loved to have played for Scotland. I must admit, the whole episode is one which I still feel bitter about today.

Two weeks after the Standard Liege win I travelled to the old East Germany (known then as the German Democratic Republic) for that Under-21s European Championship Qualifying match. Celtic's Roy Aitken was the other over-age player in a game which was played on a pitch covered by a thick blanket of snow. My Dundee United team mate Maurice Malpas also played in a match which ended 1-1. The following day we went to Dresden to watch the first team in action. Another United team mate, Eamonn Bannon, scored in the 2-1 defeat in a team which also included Richard Gough. If I remember correctly, St Mirren's Billy Thomson had a bit of a nightmare in goal that night (the big man joined us at United the following season). Anyway, on the flight home I was sitting at the front with Gough and we had two cans of beer. Next thing Big Jock (Stein) taps me on the shoulder and says, 'That's enough.' The next day Wee Jim pulled me into the office and went off his head. He shouted, 'You better fuckin' phone (Stein) and apologise!'

'What, for *two* cans of beer? What are you on about?' He then accused me of drinking champagne when it was actu-ally three of the Liverpool players sat across from us. I'm in no doubt this was him behind the scenes telling Stein to keep an eye on me. Why hadn't Big Jock tapped Gough on the shoulder and questioned *him*? The whole thing stunk! Things really went downhill after that and, for me, this was the begin-ning of the end to my Dundee United career.

My own circumstances and that of the club's may have turned

out a whole lot different had McLean not rejected what many considered to be one of the biggest jobs in British football, manager of Glasgow Rangers. Aberdeen manager Alex Ferguson had already declined the offer and McLean was next on their 'most wanted' list. This monumental news quickly filtered down to us and I admit to being overjoyed at hearing it. I wasn't the only one. We didn't believe there was any doubt in him taking the job and accepting the huge challenge of bringing League Championship titles back to Ibrox. His assistant Wattie Smith was as good as packing his gear and ready for the off. I laughed to myself and thought, 'Thank fuck, I'll maybe get paid this week!' My broad smile soon faded however when he opted, incredibly, to stay with United. With a decision like that there was no questioning his devotion and loyalty to the club and this was later rewarded when he was made a director.

He began leaving me out of games or using me as a substitute, which inevitably resulted in me adopting a negative attitude. The weather throughout January 1984 was particularly harsh and hardly a ball was kicked. We needed games and managed to arrange one at the end of that month over in St Andrews against a university select side, St Andrews United. I didn't even bother my arse trying. Predictably, he went nuts. Line-ups were being shuffled which, as I've already pointed out, in my view affected the stability of the team. The manager clearly felt justified in his selections and the need for a big squad as we were fighting on four different fronts at one point, but it still hurt being left out at times.

In early March the big European tie arrived and I was pulled straight back in. We travelled away to Austria for our quarter-final first leg tie against Rapid Vienna. They were a very good side who would prove a massive challenge to us.

Starky got the vital away goal, and what a goal it was in a 2-1 defeat which meant we were still in with a great shout of progressing, *if* we could do the business at Tannadice. Davie Dodds delivered the goods and we held onto a 1-0 victory and a place in the semi-finals of the European Cup! Obviously, the feeling in the camp was one of elation but personally it didn't grab me, not really. I was still pissed off at the way I was being treated. The fines continued for what were, at times, ridiculous offences.

A week after the Rapid tie we went out of the Scottish Cup to a defeat by our great north east rivals Aberdeen. We were still in the running for the League as well as the European Cup, but sustaining the challenge on both these fronts was going to be a very tall order. Our form was up and down but we did manage to boost morale with a 5-2 hammering of Dundee at Dens. We would need all the morale, self belief and good luck we could muster for we had drawn the Italian giants AS Roma in our semi with the first leg to be played at Tannadice. This was unfortunate as we much preferred the first leg away where we were always confident of grabbing a priceless away goal.

Anticipation among our fans was intense and the match was sure to be a sell out. Some time prior to the tie I was sitting in the kitchen at Tannadice with Luggy having a roll and a cup of tea. This was an age way before diets were considered to be of any great importance and players were given culinary delights like greasy pies. Anyway, there was only the two of us there when in came Wee Jim. There was no 'all right lads' or 'how's it going?' He ignored me completely and said to Luggy, 'I'm thinking of making it £8 and £4 for tickets. What do you think?' Luggy just agreed with him but

I piped up and said, 'Fuck that! If you can't get a tenner and a fiver for a ticket and fill this stadium for a European Cup semi final you'll *never* fill the place!'

He never said anything and walked off. Next thing the tickets were priced at a tenner and a fiver as Wee Jim and the directors had formulated an 'imaginative plan'! There was no mention of Ralph Milne's input. I should have demanded a ten per cent cut of the gate receipts! It was, of course, a big ask for the punters to part with their hard-earned dough, but it was a European Cup semi-final after all!

On the evening of 11 April 1984, in beautiful sunshine, we emerged from the tunnel into a wall of noise from the Tangerine Army; the atmosphere was immense inside a jam-packed Tannadice. The large contingent of Roma fans to our right added some friendly terrace rivalry to the occasion. We started the game in a jittery fashion and couldn't seem to find the fluid passing game which we were so capable of playing. Nerves and a healthy dose of tension had a lot to do with this and at half-time the game was still goalless, which must have suited the Italian champions no end. In the second half we came out and upped the ante, and were duly rewarded with a typical poacher's goal from Doddsy, who cracked the ball into the net from six yards. Then Starky notched with another one of his thirty-yard specials. Later I had to watch agonisingly as one of my own efforts went narrowly past the post. That would have buried them. Both teams created chances but, in the end, it stayed at 2-0, which was a great result to take over there.

Looking back now, I can't help but think how their fans must have enjoyed their trip to Dundee and savoured the welcome they received from our fans, swapping scarves and everything, even though the result didn't work out in their favour. The same can't be said in return for our own fans who had to endure the utter hell of the Olympic Stadium a fortnight later. They were indeed brave souls, each and every one of them who travelled to support us. No one connected with Dundee United who went to Italy could have dreamt beforehand just how much intimidation and infernal hatred we were about to encounter over a game of football. Sure, it *was* for a place in the final of the most prestigious club tournament in the world, but football seemed to take a back seat with this lot as the psychological war which began after the Tannadice match kicked off in earnest. After that first leg their press accused us of being on drugs!

What you have to remember was that the final was to be played in that same stadium – on their turf. There was just no way they were going to lose this game and anything and everything would be used to make sure Roma were in that final. Every piece of propaganda, every dirty trick, every low down move would be applied to ensure the desired end result.

When we arrived you could just taste the hatred. It was as intimidating as hell, which was just how they wanted it. There was certainly no red carpet and 'WELCOME TO ROME' signs to make our stay a pleasant one. The night before the game we were given sleeping tablets and the floor of our hotel was protected by armed guards, which says it all really. The surrounding streets were a no-go zone. You could just imagine a glamour continental side staying in Dundee and being holed up in one of our top hotels under the protection of an armed guard! It was just mental and, thankfully, a million miles from our own culture.

I just thought, 'Fuck all this crap! Let's get right in about them!' I really believed we could do it. On the day of the match just getting to the stadium was horrendous. Through the windows of our coach we could see the throngs of hate-filled Roma fans whipping up into a frenzied pack of baying wolves. I think this was when a few of the lads felt the bite of overwhelming fear. We were now smack bang in the centre of their hornets' nest and they didn't like it, not one little bit!

Derek Stark, one of our fullbacks, had been carrying a knee injury and wasn't fully fit but the wee man badgered (and I felt, bullied) him into declaring himself fit to play. It was to be a game too far and Starky's knee was ruined after that. So here we were, about to play in one of the biggest matches in our club's history with a man running on half tank. I'm not making any excuses, but it wasn't an ideal situation and I felt for Derek.

The Olympic Stadium was massive and the tunnel where the teams came out was situated in one of the corners. The noise was deafening. They had these huge nets up to stop missiles being thrown at the players but they still managed to pelt us with oranges. I laughed when one hit Holty right on the cheek. He picked it up and turned round to face about 20,000 screaming Italians with a look of, 'Right, who the fuck was that?' He thought better of it and dropped it, as much to say, 'I'm not fighting all of *them!*'

There were allegations after the match that the ref had been bribed but for me that theory was blown away after the third minute or so when Bruno Conti stuck the ball in the net for them. The linesman flagged offside and the ref agreed and disallowed it. I was right behind Conti and he *wasn't* offside. That's not to say there wasn't underhand tactics going on but, to be honest, the onus was on us to produce the goods and we simply never turned up. We were flat. One of the few chances, possibly the only real chance we had, fell to me.

Eamonn Bannon picked the ball up out wide and I could read Eamonn quite well, I knew when he was going to get past his marker. It was my job to get across in front of my own marker and meet the ball which he fired in at pace. I had to take it first time and, unfortunately, I skied it over the bar. Nine times out of ten I would have buried it, but it was not to be. The score was 0-0 at the time and would have put us in a great position. We then got absolutely pummelled and Roma scored the three goals they needed to reach the final. It could have been six! When we were walking off at the end I said to Gough, 'What colour was the ball?'

'White,' he replied. 'Why, what do you mean?'

'Cause I never saw it,' I said, gutted. I was playing opposite the great Brazilian Falcao. The guy was awesome, what an ability he had. For ninety minutes I became acquainted with his shadow.

What followed, however, was disgraceful and makes me sick thinking about it. A number of their players rounded on Wee Jim and were spitting on him and taunting him. It was disgusting. They ceased being football players and became stinking low-life animals! The walk back to the dressing room was hellish and little scuffles began breaking out. When we reached what we thought would be the sanctuary of the dressing room the mood became even uglier as fists and feet battered on our door. It was very intimidating and I dread to think what might have happened had we won the match. We then boarded the coach to find some of the windows had been smashed.

At the airport there was a sizeable delay as they alleged the plane was faulty and we had to wait on a spare part. All in all it was a huge relief when we did eventually take off and leave that all behind. The next night we had to attend a dinner in Dundee which was the last place any of us wanted to be. It was such a massive downer; no one was in any mood to talk about it. Until writing this book, I have never really spoken of the events of that second leg and, like Wee Jim, I too have never seen any footage of the game. It seemed the best place for those distasteful memories was the very back and darkest corners of my mind. However, I can say, like the other lads, I've played in the semis of the European Cup. It is scant consolation though for what might have been. We would have faced Liverpool in the first ever all-British final and a Scotland v England scenario at that. Sadly, those thoughts remain only in dreams.

On reflection I think we were let down in many ways by our manager. Without wishing to sound bitter or too critical, I believe we were ill-prepared for that match and I feel he lost his bottle when we touched down in Rome. It was a heart-breaking end to what had been a truly magical adventure. On the home front, I don't think he played me again that season. Having been dropped and watching him reshuffle the team I honestly couldn't wait to get out the door. We had lost our way in the League title race and only managed third spot behind Celtic and a massive ten points behind champions Aberdeen. With the combination of the Scotland non call-up and the European situation (when I felt used after having been dropped) I finished season 83/84 deflated. Those events weighed heavily on my mind and dented my confidence and self-belief. I needed to give myself a kick up the arse and get back a positive mindset.

8

INJURY AND APATHY

I actually felt rejuvenated at the beginning of season 84/85.
I'd decided to put the previous season's experiences well and
truly behind me and come out fighting. My own pre-season
training had gone well and I was feeling fit and raring to go.
Before the season kicked off, we went on a two week tour of
West Germany and Switzerland. Our first game was against
the equivalent of a pub team (so we thought) with a somewhat primitive set-up facility-wise. We got absolutely
murdered 4-0! Wee Jim was pulling what was left of his hair
out!

When the game ended we went back to their clubhouse
and were made very welcome, sitting in typical German
style around a huge table. They had a great spread laid on
with pig roast and steins of beer, it was fantastic. Well until
Wee Jim came in, that is. 'Eat your food then get on the bus
– no beer!' he ordered. Our hosts had gone to great lengths
to make sure we were well catered for and had put in a lot
of effort. His actions were downright rude to say the least.
Sadly, during the tour our charismatic and long-serving
chairman Johnston Grant passed away and the manager had

to fly home to Scotland. Wattie Smith was left in charge of the squad.

The next two games were again against what we would term 'lesser opposition' and ended in a draw and another defeat. Then came the real challenge – FC Cologne. We were all right up for this one, no more pub teams. Playing in goal for them was the controversial figure of Harald Schumacher. Two years earlier, during the semi-finals of the 1982 World Cup in a match with France, he infamously flattened one of their players with an horrendous challenge. The incident was still fresh in everyone's minds as we took to the field and, predictably, a moment arose during play when my heart went in my mouth. I floated in a cross to the near post and watched in horror as Luggy went racing in to meet it with his head, just as big Schumacher was charging out. With the latter's reckless capabilities very much to the forefront of my thoughts, I silently begged Luggy to abort his mission. There was no need to worry, however, as he nipped in and glanced the header into the empty net. What a relief and what a goal! We beat them 2-1. The tour was completed with another three matches and another two forgettable results.

On the Wednesday before the League campaign kicked off, a testimonial match was arranged for Jim McLean in recognition of his loyalty and long service to Dundee United. I guess it was a big 'thank you' as well from the club for not deserting Tannadice and taking the lucrative Rangers job.

Brian Clough, managerial giant of English football and a beautifully colourful, outspoken character, brought his Nottingham Forest side north to provide the opposition. In terms of football, Cloughie and Wee Jim were similar characters in that they'd achieved extraordinary things with provincial clubs and little resources with which to work. They were also both hard taskmasters. There the similarities ended, however as, off field, it was no secret that Cloughie liked a wee bevvy while Jim was teetotal. The day before the game I was playing tennis with my girlfriend and managed to crack myself in the head with the racket. This resulted in a cut to my eye which needed stitched at the hospital. I phoned the manager to tell him what had happened and he flew off the handle. He accused me of fighting and fined me a week's wages. To this day he still doesn't believe me, but that is exactly what happened. Anyway, he asked me if I was fit to play to which I answered, 'Of course I am, it's only a cut!' I'm not being boastful but I had another of those nights when everything just clicked and turned in a very good performance, grabbing both the goals in an entertaining 2-0 win.

After the match they opened the Jim McLean Suite and we mingled with the Forest lads, some of whom I knew from my involvement with the Scotland Under-21s and through travelling with the full squad. The big snooker table was covered over and laden with a fine selection of snacks and savouries. I spotted Richard Gough, who was standing on the other side of this table, chatting away to Brian Clough. He shouted me over and introduced me to the legendary manager. I said, 'Pleased to meet you Mr Clough. It's a pleasure to be in your presence.'

He replied, 'Good goals young man, good goals. Good game tonight.'

One of their players, Colin Walsh, then spoke to me and asked how I was getting on. The next morning, our physio, Andy Dickson stood waiting at the door for me coming in. 'Ralph, office!' he ordered. My mind was racing as I headed up to the manager's office wondering what the hell I had done now. Had someone shopped me for having a bevvy after the game? I had scored two goals and secured a win for his testimonial, surely the signs were good for once. I opened the door and was greeted with a verbal 4 x 2 baton in the face.

'See you ya wee c***! You're goin' fuckin' nowhere, I'm tellin' ya – nowhere!' He started throwing things and losing it big time.

'What are you on about?' I asked, dumbfounded.

'Do you think I'm fuckin' stupid? Cloughie fuckin' tapped you didn't he, you and your big mate (Gough)?'

Eventually I just said, 'You've got it all wrong,' and walked out the door. I hung out of the dressing room window and waited on Richy appearing, just to forewarn him of the Wee Man's foul mood. When he did arrive, I shouted as quietly as I could and alerted him to the situation. Richy just screwed up his face and said, 'I'm not going to Forest. I'm not going anywhere.'

I must have talked to Brian Clough for a minute and a half and in that time we'd allegedly struck a deal. It was mental, completely insane! Quite honestly, my feelings by then were that if he *had* come in for me, I would have left in a shot, no second thoughts. My relationship with the manager was growing ever more strained, it was becoming unbearable.

A familiar pattern was now unfolding and I wasn't being handed as many starts as in some of the previous seasons, but the same old story emerged when the European ties began. I think McLean knew I could do the business on the big stage and so, when the chips were down for the second leg of our first round UEFA Cup tie against AIK Stockholm, I duly delivered the goods. Trailing 1-0 from the away leg, we turned the screw at Tannadice and scored three with no reply. I managed to notch a brace and when the second hit the net my thoughts wandered towards the dugout and to McLean with, 'Here's what I can do when you play me.'

Three days later though, things took a turn for the worse when I suffered a bad hamstring pull whilst playing against Dumbarton at Tannadice. I landed on the deck in a sitting position and next thing the ball's played straight at me. All I could do was head it to one of our players. The fans were applauding this unorthodox move and didn't realise I'd injured myself. They must have thought they had a comedian on board and wondered what the hell I was playing at. Thinking back, it was quite a comical scene. That was me out for the next three games then Wee Jim asked if I was fit to play in the second round of the UEFA Cup. We were drawn away to the Austrian outfit Linz. I knew I wasn't fit but I said I'd give it a run and see how it went. I was running on about eighty per cent and not pushing the boat out too much. We got a great 2-1 victory and Wee Jim was over the moon.

Four days later we were due to play Rangers yet again in the final of the League Cup. Wee Jim kept at me, 'Are you fit? Are you fit?' It was very much like the situation in which Starky found himself against Roma. In my heart I knew the answer only too well but declared myself fit. The match kicked off and, to be honest, I think I was deliberately avoiding the ball, hoping not to put too much strain on the injury early on. This of course was a huge handicap to the team and there's no way they could have carried me through that whole match. With around ten minutes gone and possibly my first kick of the ball, my dodgy hamstring just snapped. It was in the area directly under my arse check and was absolute agony.

I knew it was a bad one and had to be stretchered off the field immediately.

After the game (which we lost 1-0) Wee Jim approached me in his usual friendly manner and asked, 'Were you fuckin' fit?' There was no point in saying anything. It was only the end of October and I realised I'd be sidelined for ages. The real sickener was missing out on our third round UEFA Cup tie. After a demolition job at home to Linz, we were drawn against the English giants Manchester United. Back then they weren't nearly as potent a force as they are these days but overcoming them would still prove a huge challenge with many international stars such as Gordon Strachan, Bryan Robson and Jesper Olsen gracing their team. The lads did themselves proud in the first leg at Old Trafford and returned to Dundee with a very credible 2-2 draw. The general feeling was we'd take them at Tannadice but they produced a battling performance and won the match 3-2, dumping us out of the cup. Those were two matches I would have loved to have been involved in.

Throughout the course of the season there were many changes in first team personnel as McLean looked for the right blend to gel into a solid unit. The team which had been built up in the early 80s culminating in the eventual League Championship success and which had also come so close to reaching the European Cup final, was slowly beginning to disintegrate.

My rehabilitation and fightback to fitness took somewhere in the region of four months. All I could do was turn up daily at the club and push some weights then very gradually work on my mobility. It was so serious at the time there was talk of operating on it but there's no way I was having any of that.

Hamstring operations were unheard of and I'm sure they still don't do them. To be honest I never really regained my full fitness or sharpness for the remainder of that season. I was used very sparingly and doubt if I featured in more than a handful of games. Something which did get my back up during my injury period was the issue of payment. Some players when they were injured on first team duty still received full wages *and* the bonus payments. *I was lucky to get my wages.*

As with the previous season, we finished third in the League behind Celtic, and winners for the second year in a row, Aberdeen. This meant that, for the past three seasons, the title had been won outside of the Old Firm, a feat which will probably and sadly, never be repeated. We did have one last game to play that season – the showcase Scottish Cup final against Celtic. The game had the added glamour of being the 100th to be contested in that competition and the fans, clubs and media anticipated a cracker being served up. Since the late 70s and the winning of the League Cup in 1979, Dundee United had grown in stature, ability and confidence and apart from winning the League title, had undoubtedly proved what great knockout specialists they were in cup competitions. The Scottish Cup, however, was still missing from the Tannadice trophy cabinet and the feeling was that *this* could be the year at the third time of asking.

The manager brought me back into the fold for the final and gave me a place in the starting line-up. When we went 1-0 up through a Stuart Beedie strike in the second half it seemed our prayers were being answered and the so-called 'Hampden Hoodoo' (so named after our repeated inability to win a trophy at the national stadium) would be booted into touch. We just couldn't find that telling second goal which would arguably have killed them off and, with typical never-say-die attitude, Celtic fought back and scored two goals late on. A Cup win would have put a huge smile on my face (not to mention everyone else connected with the club) and restored some of my enthusiasm after what had, for the most part, been a dreadful season. Alas it wasn't to be and, once again, Hampden became our graveyard leaving us with the 'what might have been' syndrome and another hard luck story.

9

GAME OVER AT TANNADICE

The sands of fate which had begun to trickle through the hourglass the previous season or two, now started to gather momentum and flow more steadily. My Dundee United career was in irretrievable decline and, looking back now, I'm not sure if there was anything I could have done which would have reversed this. I loved United but the stark reality was that my personality clashed too much with Jim McLean's and, in that scenario, there was only ever going to be one winner. I refused to change the person I was and he knew I wouldn't back down to his tyrannical ways. The result was fewer and fewer first team games and, for my part, a strengthening bitterness towards him. It didn't make for a healthy, professional relationship. In his book *Jousting With Giants* he harped on about me not having the correct attitude for the game. He's entitled to his opinion and I'm entitled to mine and the truth is his actions behind the scenes just wore me down.

Before the 85/86 season kicked off, I married my fiancée Kim. Pre-season training had been well underway and most of the hard work was completed. We'd got married on the Thursday and he (McLean) was expecting me in for training on the *Friday!* I just thought, 'No way, you're not doing this to me.' We went through to Edinburgh for the night and spent the rest of the day there. I was on basic wages at the time and received a wedding present of £50 from my manager. I felt like giving it back to him. I ended up sticking it on a horse in a bookie shop in Edinburgh. Willie Carson did the business at something like 7-2 and we hit the pub with the winnings.

That season the team went through more transition as Wee Jim sought to rebuild his side into one capable of continuing the challenge for top honours. For a large part of it I was restricted to the toil and grind of reserve football. I was only in my mid-twenties and this certainly wasn't where I wanted to be. I had loads more to offer Dundee United.

My involvement during our short run in the UEFA Cup provided a welcome distraction to what was happening on the domestic front. After negotiating our way past Bohemians Dublin with a relatively comfortable win, the second round saw us drawn against a team from Macedonia called Vardar Skopje, who actually played in the Yugoslavian league. Two-nil up from our home leg, we travelled away to their country where the poverty and destitution was all too noticeable. The place seemed dreary and desperate, like so many of the old Eastern bloc communist countries at that time. We drew the match 1-1 and were happy to leave the place behind. The following season they made history and became the first and, subsequently, only Macedonian team ever to win the First League amid claims of alleged match-fixing irregularities which saw many of the accused Yugoslavian teams begin that campaign with minus six points.

We crashed out of the next round to Swiss team Neuchatel

Xamax. Strangely, this was the team which my mate Davie Dodds was to end up signing for at the end of the season. Doddsy, for so long a top performer and prolific goalscorer for United, had reached the end of his contract and felt the need to move on. It seemed a very odd choice but, shortly after that particular move, he signed for United's great rivals Aberdeen, which must have pissed Wee Jim off no end!

Another of the League-winning side saw his United career end that season too, but it wasn't through choice. Our ever-present goalie Hamish McAlpine was forced to call it a day after a bad injury cut short his fantastic career. It was a sad day indeed and the Shed Boys were left without a conductor to lead off the singing. His deputy, big Billy Thomson, was to prove a very worthy custodian of the 'gloves' though, during the coming seasons. Our assistant manager and United stalwart Wattie Smith, who had served the club for what seemed like forever, also left for pastures new shortly after being made a director at United. He joined Souness at Rangers and the rest is history.

My own limited League appearances were all the more frustrating when you look at our final League placing of third. It was undoubtedly the nearest Dundee United had come to lifting the Premier League title for a second time and over-shadowed the pre-83 best effort of season 78/79. Celtic, Hearts and ourselves had been involved in a dogfight during the final run-in. With a month of the campaign still to go it seemed we had let our chance slip when we were hammered 3-0 at home from Hearts and slipped five points behind them.

However, statistics show that had we not lost crazy points in our second and third last games to Clydebank and St Mirren, after defeating Aberdeen at Pittodrie, the title flag would almost certainly have flown at Tannadice once more. With us removed from the race, the season ended sensationally when Hearts, who only needed a draw against our arch derby rivals Dundee at Dens Park, were beaten in an Albert Kidd inspired victory. I can't help but look back now and feel that I could have contributed that little extra which was needed to win the title had I been given a sustained run in the team.

Before the football season ended properly, there was the small matter of the World Cup finals which were being held in Mexico. I don't have to explain how much it would have meant to me to be there taking part on the biggest football stage on the planet. Still, five of my team mates had been selected by Scotland caretaker boss Alex Ferguson. Fergie had taken over after the sudden and tragic death of legendary figure Jock Stein and had in some ways broken the West Coast stranglehold. The fact that five players from a provincial club like Dundee United had been selected for the squad was an unbelievable achievement. Selfishly and unashamedly, I wished it had been six! The five who did United proud were Davie Narey, Paul Sturrock, Eamonn Bannon, Richard Gough and Maurice Malpas.

That close season was definitely the lowest point of my entire United career and, as I was only on basic wages, I actually had to take a job in a packaging factory to try and make ends meet. I was struggling to pay our mortgage and I ended up having to sell my car as well. The job was very basic, driving about in a forklift and performing general labour tasks for which I was paid buttons. It also involved shift work. By now I'd chucked in the towel and when I finished a shift at ten I'd head off down to the Sands nightclub in the Ferry and hit the drink. It was probably during that period when I knew things were going to go wrong.

There was a surprise in store for me one day when I went through to Glasgow Airport to pick someone up and noticed my team mate Richy Gough standing in the queue to fly to London with Dundee United Vice Chairman George Grant. I tapped him on the shoulder and said, 'Where are you going?' George seemed startled with a look of, 'What are *you* doing here?'

Richy just came right out with it and said, 'Ralph, what do you think, Tottenham or Chelsea?'

I offered my honest opinion and said, 'I wouldn't even speak to Chelsea at the moment.' They were falling apart at that time and it would have been a foolish move. Richy had made no secret of his wish to go on to better things and opted for Tottenham shortly after the 86/87 season got under way. George Grant was a lovely man and I remember an occasion when he invited us all down to the bowling club at Broughty Ferry for a few games against the locals. We shared some laughs and stories with them and had a few pints and he didn't mind at all.

The clock was now counting down and throughout the latter half of 1986 I only made seven League starts, playing mostly for the reserves. In keeping with the past few seasons, McLean saw fit to bring me back in for the big European nights. We were drawn away to French club RC Lens for our first round, first leg tie and were very lucky to escape with only a 1-0 defeat. They gave us a bit of a doing over there. Before the return leg I received an injury from one of our own players during a training stint. Chris Sulley had been brought in from Bournemouth and part of his contract went along the lines of 'if you make twenty or thirty first team appearances, you'll get the other half of your signing-on fee.' He was planning to buy a house but I told him, 'Don't bother, you'll only get nineteen games.'

Anyway, we were in training one morning and Wee Jim had been at him saying that he wasn't hard enough on the field. Well he must have taken this on board and as we both went in for a tackle, he booted me right into the air. I landed with a right clatter and smacked my elbow off my hip bone. The elbow flared up like a balloon. I was taken initially to the local hospital then up to a specialist at Bridge of Earn near Perth. Both had agreed there was nothing they could do but wait for the swelling to go down. Wee Jim was desperate to have me fit for the return leg with Lens. I declared myself fit and scored the first goal then was clean through on the keeper but, instead of shooting myself, I squared it for Tommy Coyne who slotted it into the net. We won 2-1 on aggregate. Three days later, however, myself and Tommy found ourselves relegated to the subs bench and I just thought, 'Fuck this! He really is taking the piss now!' The following match he left us on the bench again and, as we weren't used, we only got half the win bonus each. He just seemed to be making it up as he went along.

Tommy was sold a few months later to our Dark Blue neighbours across the road. Wee Jim thought he was doing well recouping his money with a £75,000 sale, but their gain was certainly United's loss. At Dundee, Tommy's career really took off and he started banging the goals in over the next few seasons. His excellent goalscoring record didn't go unnoticed and Celtic eventually snapped him up. There's no doubt, being freed of the McLean shackles did play a major part in Tommy's transformation. I felt sorry for him at United. Wee Jim had him petrified; he was a bag of nerves. On the training ground he would stick the ball in the net but come Saturday, he often struggled with the manager's words of 'encouragement'.

I remember one time McLean actually brought in a hypnotist to help Tommy and me improve our game. He pulled us into the office; this was about half-three in the afternoon, and sat us down with this Wurzel Gummidge lookalike. In between trying not to burst out laughing I kept looking at my watch thinking, 'I could do with a pint.' The guy was deadly serious as he did his bit. I just couldn't believe it!

We drew a Romanian team called Universitatea Craiova for the next round of the UEFA Cup and eventually ground out a comfortable 3-0 win at home. The return match was played in the early afternoon and, apart from losing 1-0, the only memorable incident was when Luggy got absolutely melted in a challenge from their keeper. Thankfully, after a brief delay, Luggy managed to stagger to his feet, clear his head and play on. Romania was a horrible place though and certainly not a country I'd rush back to visit.

The writing was now on the wall and the final countdown to my days at Tannadice had begun. Following the Craiova game I'm pretty certain I never played in the League, then in late November I was pulled in for the UEFA first leg home tie against Hajduk Split. We did what was required and took a 2-0 victory over to Yugoslavia for the return. The match ended 0-0 but during it I remember Kevin Gallacher being clean through. All he had to do was square the ball to me for a simple tap-in but he opted to shoot and blew it. This was significant in the fact that, had I scored, I would have taken my European goal tally to sixteen and equalled the legendary Jimmy 'Jinky' Johnstone's total. That would have meant so much to me to be 'up there' with someone like Jinky. His record was achieved over sixty-six appearances whereas mine was done over forty-two. I didn't know it at the time but I would never get the chance to equal or better Jinky's record. This was my last ever competitive venture into Europe. Still, it's a Dundee United record of which I am very proud.

At the end of that match we came back out for a warm-down and, in bizarre scenes, we were joined by some of the Hadjuk fans. During the game they had lit bonfires on the terraces and set off fireworks and some of them were still there when we reappeared. As we jogged around the pitch they decided to have a warm-down of their own and ran with us. I think they thought we were taking part in a lap of honour. Thankfully, there was no aggro or animosity from them.

The war of attrition between manager and player continued. By now, I was totally pissed off and had lost interest. On one occasion whilst training he (McLean) suspected my mood was a negative one and that I wasn't applying myself 100%. He instructed our physio Bill Ramsay to punish me with ten 200 yarders (sprints). I deliberately jogged through the lot of them just to make a point. My thinking was, 'you're not making me do any more, you're not playing me, you're treating me badly and I'm on basic wages.' Enough was enough. I was on a major low and I admit I was hitting the bevvy.

People may point the finger and say, 'Surely your fitness was suffering,' but my fitness, I felt, was never in any doubt. We were weighed every morning to see if we'd been drinking and if we were so much as a pound overweight it had to be burned off by the following day or you'd be threatened with the docking of a week's wages. Big Clarkie (John Clark), like me, was always getting it in the neck and I remember one occasion when I was all alone in the training room with the scales in front of me. I pottered about with them and eventually figured out how to 'joey' them.

I told Clarkie if he stood on one foot with the other one pressed against the middle support, the weight registered lower and he'd be in the clear. I don't know if the big man ever tried it though. John was a great character and it makes me laugh when I recall the times warming up with him before a match. As anyone who played with or against him will know, he was a big strong lump of a man who could shift over the ground as well. We used to form into groups of five and play a game called BIFF. You had to play the ball first time and if it went a few yards either side of your team mate you got a B and so on, a bit like the game DONKEY. The trouble was, when Big Clarkie was in the group a 'light tap' from him came at you like an Exocet missile!

In January 1987, Charlton Athletic tabled a bid for me. Wee Jim weighed up his options and approached one of our directors Doug Houston for his opinion. He basically told McLean to let me go as I wasn't doing it (performing) on the pitch. I was going to send Doug a couple of hundred quid as a thank you. It was definitely a case of 'get me out of here'. I'll state again, I had no wish to leave Dundee United but my hand was forced. In some ways, and maybe with the benefit of hindsight, I wish I'd never left, but I did and I had to get on with it. I had a wife, a mortgage and bills to pay like everyone else, but the struggle from living mostly on reserve wages was too much.

On the Tuesday leading up to the Charlton offer being made official, Wee Jim offered me a new contract. He brought me in for a chat, but I already had wind of the Charlton interest.

When he discussed a new contract I told him I didn't want one because I already had one for about forty years! He offered me a five grand signing-on fee but I declined it.

'I know what some of the others got,' I said. He went completely off his nut!

'How the fuck do you know what they got?' he raged.

'They all got £25,000 each.'

'That's because they're internationalists,' he argued.

'Yeah, and you stopped me from being an internationalist!'

'Right, you want twenty-five grand; you go out there and do it for me.'

I said to him to give me the money and I would go out and do it for him. There was a stalemate and neither of us would budge.

I had a foot injury at the time and the reserves were playing on the Friday night. I don't know if McLean thought I was faking it or not but it was a sore one and I couldn't put all my weight onto it. However, every Friday morning there was a board meeting and following that, McLean phoned me in the evening to ask if I was coming down to the reserve match. I said I wasn't. He continued, 'Well, I wasn't going to say anything but I might as well tell you. There's an offer come in from Charlton Athletic and the board have decided to accept it.'

'You mean *you've* decided to accept it!' He just blanked that comment and told me a guy called Arnie Warren would be in contact soon and put the phone down. Both clubs had obviously agreed a fee but at that point I was unaware. To be honest I really wasn't caring. At that point I think he felt he'd finally won the battle of the wits between us, but the truth of it was he'd lost a bloody good player.

When Arnie phoned he explained the difficulty he had in dealing with McLean and trying to get an answer out of him. It was arranged for me to fly to London on the Sunday morning where I would be met by one of their club representatives. On the Saturday morning I went into Tannadice and received some treatment on my injured foot from a new physio we had. He then told me to put my kit on and have a jog around the track. I told him in no uncertain terms 'where to go'. He was panicking. When he threatened to phone Wee Jim I asked one of the young players to go and collect my boots from the boot room. That was it, I was off. I don't know if the physio realised I was winding him up but it didn't matter anyway, I knew I was on my way out.

Before I departed Jim McLean informed me of a phone call which he'd received a few years earlier from the then Rangers manager Jock Wallace. Jock had enquired about my availability some time after we'd won the League and how much it would cost to take me to Rangers. He was told unequivocally by Wee Jim that I was not for sale. Jock persisted and eventually drew a response from McLean. 'OK, you can have Ralph Milne in a straight swap for Ally McCoist.' The future 'Super' Ally had not long signed and Wee Jim knew this would be an impossible demand. Jock Wallace also knew this and told him so. Ralph Milne was going nowhere. Around this period Willie Waddell of Rangers had stated in the press that I was the best winger in Scotland and should be playing for the national side and his opinions were well respected.

A few years later (when I was with Man United), I bumped into Jock in a hotel in Southampton so I asked him for his side of the story regarding the Rangers interest. He said, 'We were desperate to get you there but he [McLean] just messed me about from the start. I would never ever try and do a deal with him again!'

I make no apologies for raising issues which concerned my relationship with Jim McLean and how I perceived them. However, it is not my intention to get into a slanging match with a tit-for-tat volley of claims and counter claims. What's done is done. I would like to end this chapter though with a couple of quotes from his book *Jousting With Giants*.

He was a typical example of the attitude I talked about earlier – when things went wrong Ralph would look around and blame everyone but himself. That was always his way. Everyone at the club knew that and I think maybe the fans learned to recognise it as well. They never did like him. I would doubt if there were many tears shed on the terracings when he finally left to join Charlton. He could have achieved so much more but when the big demands were made Ralph was often posted missing.

If I had an outstanding failure then it was with Ralph Milne. He should have been playing in World Cups. He should have won a bundle of Scotland international honours. It was a tragedy that the boy was not playing for his country all the time. He had tremendous talent – and I failed with him. He did not have the right attitude to the game and I could not instil that into him. If I had more Milnes to deal with then I would have been out of a job. I see him as a failure for me personally.

I'll let you make up your own minds.

10

A FRESH START GOES PEAR-SHAPED

I flew down to London on the Sunday morning minus any 'good luck wishes' from Mr McLean, not that I'd expected any. When I arrived I was taken to a plush hotel and told I'd be going to the ground the following morning. However, we weren't going to Charlton's home park 'The Valley' as the Football League had closed it over safety issues the previous season. Charlton were playing their home ties at Crystal Palace's ground Selhurst Park. As a club I knew virtually nothing about them or their history. As it transpired, they were in a bit of financial turmoil at the time but I didn't care, it was a change of scenery. Charlton paid Dundee United £125,000 for my services and that night we agreed terms and I signed the contract.

The fact I was carrying a foot injury played on my mind and I was worried that the deal might still fall through. I did not relish the thought of having to go back to Tannadice. They arranged a medical and the club paid for me to be seen by a specialist at Harley Street, which must have cost them a fortune. Thankfully, the guy gave me the all-clear and assured my new employers the injury would heal up.

At the time Charlton were playing in the English First Division (which was the top flight), having gained promotion only the season before. Although hailing from London, they were by no means one of the glamour clubs but did boast a decent-sized following. When I joined they were struggling in the lower reaches of the League and were probably tipped by many to go straight back down again. Hopefully, that wasn't going to be the case and I could do my bit to help the cause.

Not long after I'd gone down south the draw was made for the quarter-finals of the UEFA Cup. Dundee United were paired with the Catalan giants of world football, Barcelona. To say I was gutted would be a massive understatement! It really did leave me with a sick feeling inside. I would have loved to have been in that line-up to face Terry Venables' star-studded side which included Brits Gary Lineker and Mark Hughes. At that stage Dundee United were the only British team left in all European competitions and the eyes of the nation were fixed firmly upon them.

On the night of 4 March 1987 I watched with millions of others as United pulled off a stunning victory to take a 1-0 lead to the famous Nou Camp. Two weeks later they achieved the unthinkable and defeated the Spaniards 2-1 on their own turf and in doing so repeated the club's performance of 1966 when they won home and away in the old Fairs Cup. Until very recently, they still held the record of being the only British side to have won in Spain, and not just once, but twice!

They followed that historic victory with a semi-final win over old sparring partners Borussia Moenchengladbach and so became the first Scottish team to reach the final of the UEFA Cup. I was extremely proud of their magnificent efforts, if not a little envious. Unfortunately, they narrowly lost out on lifting the cup at Tannadice to Swedish team Gothenburg with a 2-1 aggregate score. I don't mind admitting I was convinced we would have won that game had I still been there. I always had the buzz for the European games, always right up for it. Yes it's a big claim, but I honestly believe I could have provided the extra magical spark needed on such an occasion. I know one person for sure who will disagree with that!

My foot injury was still giving me some bother but our manager Lennie Lawrence asked me to go and have a run-out on the Selhurst Park pitch (which was frozen) to see how I fared. We were due to face Manchester United in a League game and I told Lenny I was fine, no problems. It was of course a wee white lie as it was still giving me jip, but I was desperate to play. I remember having a laugh at the top of the tunnel with Fergie and his assistant Archie Knox (whom I knew from his days at Dundee United). Anyway, the ref gave the pitch the all-clear and I took the field for my debut against the mighty Red Devils. It was very much a case of headless chickens chasing shadows though and we got humped 4-0. Welcome to Charlton!

The club had moved me to a hotel in Blackheath in order to give me a chance to settle into my new surroundings. This was only meant to be for a three month period but they very kindly gave me an extension to this rule due to our involvement in the end of season play-offs. My wife Kim had stayed behind in Dundee as we still had the house in the Ferry but, again, the club were generous and allowed her six flights for visits. This wasn't an ideal situation for our marriage (or for any marriage) but we just had to get on with it as best we could in the meantime.

Once I got to know the lads I did take advantage of this

'freedom' and partook in some bevvy sessions in the local hostelries. They were a great bunch of guys and one of their players, Colin Walsh, I already knew from the Scotland Under-21s. There were two other Scots also down there at the time, Mark Reid and Jim Melrose. Mark was an ex-Celtic player whom I'd tussled with on occasion back in the Scottish Premier Division. Walshy, Mark and me soon formed a tight-knit little group and were always having a laugh and taking the piss out of ourselves and the others. The stand-out in the team was Rob Lee who was a great player and it was no surprise when he went onto bigger things playing for Newcastle and England.

At the end of March 1987 we reached the final of the Full Members Cup (or Simod Cup as it was also known) and were due to face Blackburn Rovers. This competition was created the previous season to give English clubs something else to play for following their European ban after the Heysel Stadium disaster. Although it was only a minor cup, it was a fantastic occasion to be involved in, especially as it was played at the famous Wembley Stadium. I remember hitting a terrific screamer of a shot which just blazed over the bar with the score still locked at 0-0. Unfortunately, we were defeated 1-0 and their goalscorer was none other than big Colin Hendry, who had not long signed from Dundee FC.

There was another Dundee connection too in the form of Rovers' manager Donald MacKay. Donald had served Dundee United as a keeper for ten years during the 60s and early 70s. And he was of course the manager of the Dundee side we defeated with United to win the League on that historic day in 1983. Also on that opposing side was ex-United player Chris Sulley, the same guy who had up-ended me and wrecked my elbow in training after taking Wee Jim's advice of 'not being hard enough'.

I found it hard to get any kind of run in the team as Lennie's philosophy was if the team was winning or even drawing he was loathe to change things around. When I did get the chance I usually turned in a decent performance. We were due to face fellow strugglers Aston Villa on the May Day Bank Holiday Monday and Lennie asked the players if anyone would like to go and stay in the hotel at Croydon on the Sunday night. Villa were managed by Celtic legend Billy McNeill at the time, who had quit Manchester City earlier in the season to become boss. Billy must have felt like he'd jumped out of the frying pan and into the fire though when the season ended disastrously for him. Anyway, Walshy and I took up Lennie's offer and decided to have a slap-up meal when we got there. Both of us pondered over what to have from the menu then I broke the silence and said, 'I think I'll have the soup followed by a big steak.'

'Yeah, I'll go for some of that as well.'

The soup was gazpacho which, for those who don't know, is a Spanish dish served cold. I sat back and relaxed, trying hard not to laugh at the impending outcome. The waiter delivered the soup so I waited, had a taste then said, 'Walshy, this soup's not very warm, how's yours?'

He tasted it then said, 'Mine's fuckin' freezing!' I told him to get the waiter back over which he did. 'You can take that back mate,' he ordered.

The waiter replied, 'Is there something wrong with it sir?'

'Yeah, it's bloody freezing!'

'It's supposed to be like that sir.'

Walshy glanced over to see me pissing myself laughing and

gave me a few boots under the table. He eventually saw the funny side of it.

As the season drew to a conclusion it became evidently clear that we were struggling to stay in the First Division and were involved in what was probably a five or six team scrap for survival. Three teams would be going straight down and whoever finished fourth bottom would have to battle it out in a play-off against sides from Division Two. This was the first season in which this format was to be used. It was tense stuff and as most football fans and players alike will tell you, football at the wrong end of the table is not very pretty to watch. In the end, Aston Villa, Manchester City and Leicester City took the drop and we finished in the dreaded fourth bottom spot. Derby County and Portsmouth were promoted from Division Two which left Oldham Athletic, Leeds United, Ipswich Town and ourselves scrapping for the last Division One place. Over two legs we overcame Ipswich while Leeds disposed of Oldham, setting up a two-leg final with the men from Yorkshire.

In the first game at Selhurst Park we were leading 1-0 and I came on as a sub. With about a minute left on the clock Leeds player Micky Adams elbowed me in the face and broke my cheekbone. The pain was excruciating, I'd never felt anything like that before. The physio asked me how I was and I think I must have been in cuckoo land and told him I was all right. When the ball was passed to me though I just booted it away, I didn't want anyone near me. The fans came on the pitch to celebrate and all I could do was try to keep them away from my cheek. I don't know if the elbow was a deliberate one or not but Micky Adams never came to see me after the game to apologise. It didn't look good on his part.

The doctor came to examine me and with tears in my eyes I asked him if he could give me something for the pain. I refused any tablets as I thought they'd make me sick so he went away for what seemed like an eternity then reappeared and gave me an injection. As we travelled by car up to Whitechapel Hospital I asked the doctor what he had given me. I told him I didn't know whether to laugh or cry and, amazingly, the pain had disappeared.

He replied, 'I've given you diamorphine. It's a wonderful drug; I can understand why people get hooked on it.'

I thought, 'Jesus Christ, hold on a minute here,' but it certainly dissolved the pain – and possibly my brain! By around eight o'clock that evening I was sitting up in bed watching TV, I felt brand new. I couldn't feel my cheek though, which was maybe just as well. The surgeons operated the next morning and the consultant had said that, because it was a standard break and not shattered, it would heal much quicker. I would however need to get the stitches out in three weeks time.

Other folk are less fortunate as a shattered cheekbone needs all sorts of rebuilding work. I was told I could leave the following day so Kim came and picked me up and took me back to the hotel. I sorted a few things out then drove all the way back to Dundee. We were booked up along with my parents to fly out and visit my uncle and auntie in America for a month's holiday. I had made sure the season would be over when doing this but didn't for a moment think we'd be involved in the play-offs. In any case I was injured and couldn't possibly have played with the facial injury.

There was a little story behind the American trip and why it had come about. When I first signed for Charlton I did an interview for the *Daily Record* and was paid a generous fee.

At the time my dad had been feeling very unwell and kept vomiting. I thought he was dying. Something he said he'd always love to do before he left this earth was to go and visit his younger brother (my uncle Ralph) in Boston. I said to him, 'Here, take this money and go. You've no excuses now. It's on one condition though – you go to the doctor's and get that lump examined.' He eventually dragged himself along to his GP's surgery and emerged with some terrible news. He told me he'd had a large lump in his mouth for years but it had never worried him. I could have strangled him! Those words which everybody dreads dropped out of his mouth and landed like an anvil on my heart – 'It's cancerous.'

I was both stunned and frightened, like anybody would be in that situation. He assured me the doctor had told him to go ahead with the holiday and they would operate when we got back. We spent a month there and, given the circumstances, mum and dad had a truly fantastic time. When we came home dad had a lengthy operation where surgeons unsuccessfully tried to burn it out. In the end they had to cut it out, which left my dad with a facial disfigurement. This knocked his confidence a bit as he was always a good-looking man. It did, however, give him another good few years of life, for which he was very grateful. That *Daily Record* article went a long way to saving my dad's life for had it not been for the chain of events which followed, it's highly likely he would have passed away much sooner.

When we were over there I'd mentioned to my uncle that I would need to get my stitches removed, which would probably have cost an arm and a leg. I was going to take them out myself if I had to but, thankfully, it didn't come to that. We were invited to a barbeque at this huge mansion which

My football career kicked off with Dundee Celtic Boys
where I had many happy and memorable times.
I'm sitting second from right.

Receiving a Player of the Year Award with Dundee Celtic
Boys from the legendary Bertie Auld. Dundee United's
John Holt and Paul Sturrock are standing behind.

Left: In action at Hampden Park during our 1981 Scottish Cup Final replay with Rangers. We were soundly beaten 4-1.

Below: September 1981. Scoring against French side AS Monaco at Tannadice during a UEFA Cup tie. We won 6-4 on aggregate and Dundee United had come of age.

14th May 1983 – history in the making. Dundee keeper Colin Kelly can only watch as my chip flies over his head and into the net on our way to winning the Premier League for the first and only time in Dundee United's history.

Hearts players Alex Macdonald and Sandy Jardine are powerless to stop this shot going net bound.

Aberdeen's Jim Leighton and Doug Rougvie watch helplessly as this rocket flies into the net at Pittodrie. This was the crucial match which we won 2-1 in March 1983 and saw us right back in the hunt for the title.

Celebrating a goal against Rangers at Ibrox.

A rare headed goal against Hearts at Tannadice.

Celebrating our title win with some young fans.

All smiles at Dens Park after our historic triumph over rivals Dundee.

UEFA Cup action at Tannadice from 1984 – scoring against AIK Stockholm.

THE FOOTBALL LEAGUE FULL MEMBERS CUP FINAL

BLACKBURN ROVERS V CHARLTON ATHLETIC

SUNDAY, MARCH 29th, 1987. KICK-OFF 3.00 p.m.

WEMBLEY
WHERE £1.15

Official Souvenir Programme £1

MATCH SPONSOR HOMES MITRE

My first and only appearance at Wembley playing for Charlton against Blackburn Rovers in the Full Members Cup Final. We lost 1-0.

My move to Charlton from Dundee United proved to be a rather unhappy one.

In action for Charlton Athletic.

Scoring in the match against
Luton at Old Trafford which was a
huge buzz.

In action for Manchester United v
Luton Town, March 1989. I scored
one of my three goals for the club
in a 2-0 victory.

Celebrating my 22nd birthday in style the day before we won the League title.

Learning to play the piano was never a popular hobby with boys in the housing schemes but I soon became a dab hand on the ivories.

With best friend Andy McPhee and Dave Narey at a function.

A very proud moment indeed when I took my mum and dad on holiday to visit relatives in America.

My youngest son Robert.

My son Bradley's first day at school.

turned out to be the home of the treasurer of my aunt and uncle's pipe band. His name was Bob Loughran and he was also a doctor. When I told him what had happened he said he'd take the stitches out for me, which was very handy and probably saved me a fortune.

The second leg at Elland Road saw Leeds secure a 1-0 victory which meant the tie would need to be decided with a third and final encounter. This game was played at the neutral venue of St Andrews, home to Birmingham City. Unfortunately, I was in America at the time and it proved to be something of a challenge trying to get the result. The anxiety and worry was obliterated though when I finally received the news that Charlton had beaten Leeds 2-1 after extra time. With a no-goal stalemate after ninety minutes Leeds drew first blood and took the lead in the first period of extra time. Charlton were heading for Second Division football until our captain, Peter Shirtliff, popped up and notched a magnificent double. He was a great guy whom I had loads of time for. His wife actually made the curtains for the house we eventually bought in London.

Towards the end of that season I had slowly and uncharacteristically been gaining weight which was affecting my fitness and play. During the close season I went on a diet and fired in about some tough training and returned for the 87/88 campaign in good shape. The guys didn't recognise me when I showed up at the club. To add to this the club decided to take the squad for a week's intense fitness with the Royal Marines down at Lympstone in Devon. When we arrived we were taken into the Sergeant's Mess and Lennie gave us a briefing.

'OK, lads listen up. I want everyone on their best behaviour while we're staying here. These guys (Marines) have been kind enough to accommodate us so let's put in maximum effort. I don't mind you having a drink but, remember, we're here for fitness.'

The first night we went down to the pub which was just outside the barrack gates. There were about a dozen of us and everyone bought a round. Our training had got off to a great start! I was rooming with Walshy and when he woke up in the morning he was in a bad way. 'Fuck me,' he groaned, 'I feel terrible.'

'Don't worry mate, I've got everything,' I said. 'It's all under control. There's the paracetamol, there's the Andrews Liver Salts, whack a load of that into you and let's go!'

The PTI (Physical Training Instructor) was already waiting and looking forward to dishing out some gruelling punishment. This is just what we needed after a heavy night. As we assembled for a short all-terrain, cross country type of run it was plain to see that everyone was suffering big time. We all made it within the designated time though. At the end I looked at Walshy and he looked at me. I asked how it was for him. All he could squeeze out was, 'I can't breathe.' It was hilarious. Next we were taken into the gym for a bout of weight training and circuits and gradually everyone came to after sweating out the toxins. In the afternoon some of us went back to our rooms and crashed out for a couple of hours. I got up and turned to my mate and said to him, 'What are we gonna do now Walshy?' He just looked at me. 'C'mon we'll go downstairs.'

We both wandered into the Sergeant's Mess and got chatting with a soldier who was a Warrant Officer 2nd Class and came from Arbroath. Sure as fate, one thing led to another and we were right on it (drinking) again. We ended up back at the same pub as the previous night and on our return we had to wait for clearance at the main gate. As we walked, or rather gracefully staggered, over to the mess a young guy called Paul Williams (whom Lennie Lawrence had just signed) clocked us whilst leaning out of his window. He didn't drink and shouted down, 'Fuck me Walshy, look at the state of you, you're hammered!' Walshy stopped me and said, 'Ralph, watch this.'

'Paul,' he called back. 'See the difference between me and you?'

'Yeah what is it?'

'About four hundred pound a week!' The two of us just cracked up laughing and left young Paul to ponder that thought. That whole week was unbelievable, we were out every night. At the end of the training Lennie was over the moon. He addressed us all and said, 'Great, everybody completed everything – brilliant! We're bang on target!'

I thought, 'Fuck me, if that had been Tannadice we'd have been banged up in solitary for three days!' It was incredible. I must admit, though, the training we received was fantastic, I really enjoyed it. They had us going through those claustrophobic concrete tunnels and under the water and all sorts. It wasn't too clever on the knees for us football players though. I was able to keep up with the PTI, always at the front. He was a great lad. I was to cross paths with some of the Marines years later when I was in Hong Kong.

Following on from our stint at Lympstone a small pre-season tour was arranged in Sweden and we stayed in a beautiful little town called Askersund. This place was truly stunning and was situated at the north of Lake Vattern. The downside was we were stuck away out in the middle of nowhere and the price for a beer was astronomical. No one wanted to drink in the hotel under the watchful eye of our management team so about twelve of us trooped off down to the town and found a little bar. We were paying some ridiculous price like £8 a pint but nobody was too bothered and we got on with it. At ten o'clock, however, the barman shut up shop and wouldn't serve us any more. This wasn't due to any shenanigans on our part; it was the official time when they stopped serving and we were all chucked out. We were prepared to pay these extortionate prices but the guy was having none of it. Back home, a barman would have bitten your hand off for that kind of business and given us a three-day lock-in! Everyone was gutted (certainly not guttered!). I thought we were back in 1972 or something. That was it; we had to go back to the hotel with our bottom lips trailing the ground.

I had a carry-on one morning when I dressed up in army fatigues, hat and all and soaked our coach Brian Eastwick with an AK47 battery-operated water-pistol in front of everyone. He said, 'Milney that was funny for about five minutes . . .' I never let him finish and opened up with another burst. Shortly afterwards I got pulled from Lennie Lawrence who said, 'Milney, the chairman says you've got to get rid of the water-pistol.'

I said, 'Is that right? Well you tell the chairman to come and tell *me* to get rid of the water-pistol because I bought that in America and it's very precious to me.' The chairman bottled it so I kept it and took it on our next trip, which nearly landed us in hot water with the local police. Whilst out there in Askersund I'm sure we played three games against minor opposition but all in all it was a great trip. From a personal point of view I didn't rate our coach Brian Eastwick at all. There were occasions when I found his training methods quite bizarre. That was one of the things I took really badly with, coming from Tannadice where the coaching was excellent.

He'd come away with commands like 'boot it into the corner' or 'stand it up in the air'. I was often left scratching my head saying, 'What the fuck does that mean?' Basically it was just 'kick it anywhere you want and chase after it'. Yeah, that will be fuckin' right! And people wonder why I never scored for them?

We then went over to Italy to play Pisa in a pre-season friendly. Big Paul Elliott (who later went to Celtic) was with them at the time. We played them on a Saturday night and got well and truly hammered. We weren't scheduled to fly back till the Monday so Lennie Lawrence told us to 'do what you want.' However, Lennie's 'do what you want' and our 'do what you want' were at the complete opposite ends of the socialising scale. We hit the town and got absolutely guttered. Back at the hotel the festivities carried on and I ended up belting out some tunes on a grand piano. I eventually slumped into bed around five in the morning, some of the others never even made their beds!

On the Sunday, Mark Stuart received the news that his wife had delivered their child so we trooped down to the beach and went right on the piss. I had the dreaded water-pistol with me so my team mate Steve Thompson borrowed it and let rip on one of the barmaids, soaking her. He thought this was hilarious. Shortly afterwards a couple of police officers arrived and when one of them pointed what looked like a machine gun at him, he nearly shat himself and dropped the toy gun. I just about ended myself with laughter. Again, we got totally plastered. By the Monday we all should have been suffering from the worst hangovers ever but carried on drinking onboard the flight and emptied the plane of champagne. That was one hell of a friendly!

That same summer I'd managed to get my house sold in Broughty Ferry to Dundee United player John Clark and his wife, which meant Kim was finally able to move down to London with me. This was a huge weight off both our shoulders as she was expecting our first child and we were able to be together. I'd bought a house in nearby Crayford down in Kent and we settled in but I wasn't happy, not for the fact that my wife was here, far from it. It was the place. I didn't like London from the moment I moved down and I was slowly beginning to detest it. I'm not sure if I was homesick, I may well have been, but it was gnawing away at me now on a daily basis. Don't get me wrong, the set up at Charlton was good and the lads especially were brilliant, but something just wasn't clicking. I wasn't enjoying my football either, which didn't help. In the four or five months I'd been down, I'd only made twelve appearances and the new season was following the same pattern. Reserve football wasn't my scene.

Shortly before Christmas of that year Kim travelled back up to Dundee to have our baby. We'd both agreed on this because the hospital in Dartford was getting a lot of bad reports at the time and I didn't want my wife in there. There was of course another factor; I didn't want our child being born in England. Meanwhile my auntie phoned me from America to tell me my cousin Heather was flying over to London from Madrid then moving on to Scotland and asked if I would pick her up. She spent a few days in the capital then I collected her and took her to Kings Cross station to catch a train.

In a bizarre twist of fate I met a guy whom I knew from my old housing scheme in Douglas and he asked if I was going home (to Dundee). He had a load of spare first class tickets (God knows where he got them) and told me to hop on. I explained I was only dropping my cousin off and that she was heading back to Douglas herself. For some odd reason, probably the pull of home, I boarded the train with them, which panicked Heather a little.

'Ralph,' she said, 'you'll have to get off.'

'Ach, the next stop's not for two hours, don't worry,' I assured her. My decision was already made in my mind though. I was staying on. The alternative was to spend Christmas alone in London while my pregnant wife was in Dundee. Added to that, I wasn't getting a game so I just thought, 'Fuck it! I'm going home!' I ended up on the bevvy with my mate for the rest of the journey.

When I got to Dundee I phoned Lennie Lawrence and told him that Kim had been taken into hospital early hence the reason I was there, but that it was a false alarm. He said, 'Look Milney, just stay up there till the baby's born.' Kim gave birth to our son Bradley shortly afterwards. I stayed a little longer than I probably should have, but the news I was about to receive in London would hit me for six.

11

WAY OUT WEST

I travelled back down south and was playing in a reserve match at Welling when our manager pulled me off at half-time and took me up the stairs. I wondered what was going on. He dropped a bit of a bombshell and said, 'Terry Cooper wants you on loan at Bristol City. You might as well go and get some match fitness cause you're not in my plans at the moment.'

I was completely taken aback by this news. I just kept saying to myself, 'Bristol, Bristol – what bloody league are *they* in?' I found out fellow Scot and legend Joe Jordan was playing there in what was the twilight of an outstanding career. I thought, 'What the hell, anything to get out of London!' I went down there and scored a cracking twenty-yard volley on my debut against Bury. Terry Cooper was sufficiently impressed and said after the match, 'I definitely want to sign you.'

On the Monday I said, 'Let's do it, get me out of London, I fuckin' hate it!' Terry advised me to see out my month's loan period as City couldn't compete with the wages I was getting with Charlton, and they were still my employers. I had accumulated twenty-two appearances over the course of a year, which was a poor showing with no goals to show for it. People often ask me why I never scored during my time with Charlton to which I reply, 'No fuckin' wonder! I'd like to see *you* score from your own penalty box! We were never out of ours!'

For that month I trained at Charlton on the Monday and Tuesday then travelled and stayed in Bristol till the Saturday. Steve McClaren (the future England boss) came to Bristol on loan from Derby County at the same time and we ended up signing contracts together. I was signed for £50,000 and I'm sure we were both on three-year deals. We'd played an away game against Southend United on the Friday night and after it I went straight back to my home in London. Half the team were struggling with a flu bug and we got beat 2-0 in a match we were really expected to win. I think Terry was in a no-win situation himself as the team weren't doing that great. This result was probably the straw that broke the camel's back for the board. The following Wednesday I went back down to Bristol and was chatting away to Stevie in the hotel digs when he stopped me and said, 'You don't know do you?'

'Don't know what?' I asked.

'Terry got the sack on Friday night!'

'You're joking, we've just signed contracts and we don't have a manager?' Terry was a sound guy and I really had a lot of respect for him. He was a very good player in his day, especially with the great Leeds side of the 60s and early 70s. He also played for and managed both Bristol City and their derby rivals Rovers. After the home games he would always give our captain Rob Newman twenty quid to buy the players a drink in the players' lounge upstairs. He would go into the boardroom with his wife first then they'd both come and join us later in the lounge. It was a great gesture and earned him the respect and friendship of the lads. He was replaced by Joe Jordan whom they made caretaker manager until the end of the season.

During this period my head was in a huge turmoil. Kim and I were going through a marriage break-up and I was in the depths of despair. She'd been down a couple of times while I was at Bristol, but it just wasn't working. I'd gone back to Dundee for my son Bradley's christening and returned south alone. I phoned her and asked when she was coming down, but she wasn't. It was all over. Those were utterly hellish times and the reality hit home hard that I wasn't going to see and be with my wife and son. The saving grace which held my sanity together were the players and coaching staff at Bristol City Football Club. It was a beautiful part of the country and the people were really friendly. This was in total contrast to London. The lads were a great bunch to work with and the coaching and training was fantastic. The whole atmosphere of the place was very welcoming and I fitted in from the moment I arrived. There was no feeling of pressure. I just knew it was right and I was getting a steady game and back enjoying my football once more.

Big Joe had worked some kind of miracle with us and took the club from a mediocre position in the Third Division to a final placing of fifth and the opportunity to compete in the promotion play-offs. I did my bit to help us into this challenging position when I struck a stunning winner (even if I say so myself!) against York City. To be honest I was having a complete stinker that day and when I received the pass from Rob Newman my first touch was so bad it went in the exact opposite direction of where I wanted it. Luckily it created an opening and I deftly chipped their keeper with my left foot from a crazy angle.

Subsequently we were drawn against Division Two opponents Sheffield United, who had been pulled into the play off scrap having finished third bottom. In the first leg we beat them 1-0 at our Ashton Gate stadium then secured a place in the final with a battling 1-1 draw away and relegated them in the process. The first leg of the final ended disastrously at home for us with a 3-1 defeat at the hands of Walsall. I'm sure it was the night before the return game that Man United were entertaining AC Milan in a glamour friendly at Old Trafford. I put it to Joe that seeing as we weren't far from Manchester he should take us to see both his former teams in action, which he very generously did.

The whole Man United team struggled that night and took a bit of a doing but to be fair to them the pitch was in a horrendous condition. Stars of the Milan side at that time included Ruud Gullit and my all-time favourite player Marco van Basten. Little did I know as I watched that game that I'd soon be involved in talks with the United manager. The next day, in our second leg against Walsall, we rolled up our sleeves and got stuck right into them at Fellows Park and won with a convincing 2-0 score.

When I had arrived at Bristol I thought, 'Great, I'll get down that wing and just float them onto the head of Joe Jordan.' Although the big man was virtually at the end of his career, he did turn out for us in this game. Our main target man was a guy called Carl Shutt, who wasn't the biggest of players. Prior to the second leg I'd said to Joe that he needed to play for us. He made an instant impression and, within the first ten minutes, had decked three Walsall players with his no-nonsense rough-house style.

I had an opportunity to get my name up in lights with a great chance which would have sealed our promotion. With only about five minutes left on the clock a cross was flighted in but, unfortunately, the sun was glaring at the back of it and, without making any excuses, it dazzled me slightly as I connected with the ball. I caught it sweet enough but it flew just over the bar. Like an angler would say, 'it was the one that got away.'

The replay was played only two days later, again at Fellows Park, but we would have been as well going swinging with the monkeys in Bristol Zoo than turning up. We were destroyed by four goals to nil. Big Joe's exertions during the second leg had taken their toll and, unfortunately, he couldn't recover quickly enough to play. I'm certain that had it been a week until the replay he would have played and we would have won, such was the influence his presence commanded. He had come so, so close to achieving something spectacular from virtually nothing, but it wasn't to be. His time would come though.

On my arrival at City I had been staying in the hotel digs but then Rob Newman kindly agreed to let me move in with him, which I greatly appreciated. My marriage break-up constantly tumbled over in my mind but Rob and the rest of the lads helped me pull through those difficult times. I really enjoyed the city and its people and, as I was in the 'single' bracket again, I was enjoying the social life as well, maybe a little too much. I tended to have a drink in the afternoon. I mean, there's just no way you could fall into bed at four in the morning and expect to get up and put in a shift at training.

My philosophy was, if you got plenty sleep, you were OK to rise in the morning and get stuck in about training. Once you get that certain level of fitness and you're still relatively young, you can usually maintain it easily. The problem for some is the actual getting fit and putting in the hard graft. That's the difficult part. Those Saturday after match sessions in the players' lounge would sometimes carry on till one or two in the morning; none of us really worried though as Sunday was a day off. Most players' lounges closed at 6pm but not ours, not the Bristol boys. They had a piano in the place and guess who ended up doing the odd turn or three on it? Yep, Ralphie Van Beethoven!

We had some mental nights in there then we'd stagger out and catch the last hour or two in the nightclubs. I'm not sure if Big Joe knew what was going on. I think it was a case of what he didn't know about he didn't worry about and just as well. Don't get me wrong though, Joe was strict and would give you a kick in the arse if you needed it, but none of the players were out of order.

I managed to get my house sold in London and made a very healthy profit from it. I'd gone from being skint eighteen months ago to now having some cash in my pocket. When we broke off for the end of that season, I decided to try and get my head together and took a short break to the island of Jersey in the Channel Islands. I still held a faint glimmer in my heart that I may be able to save my marriage but, on my return from Jersey, I was assured there would be no reconciliation. I then went on a longer break over to America, which was just what I needed. It was all very laid back and relaxing and, on my return, I felt somewhat more mentally focused.

I had a boxer dog called Jessie which Kim had taken back

to Dundee with her. The poor thing was being shipped from pillar to post so I decided to go up and collect her and bring her back down with me. Joe and his wife told me they would take her in the meantime until I got myself a new house. I drove the 450 miles and was only in Dundee for half an hour before driving straight back down. I said to Joe, 'Look, if you want Jessie take her. She's been getting messed about too much and just needs a stable home. You've got a lovely big house and garden and she'd love it here.' It really broke my heart to hand her over though. I really loved that dog, but I knew she'd be well looked after and she was.

As one door closed another opened and I met a lovely girl called Lee in the Porthouse nightclub in Bristol. We got on really well and a relationship soon blossomed.

During the close season of 88/89 Joe took us up to Largs in Scotland for some warm-up games with Kilmarnock and Morton. One night we ended up in a nightclub and were having a great time when all hell broke loose. As you can imagine, a squad of English guys taking over the place didn't go down too well, especially when one of the lads started chatting up a local girl who just happened to be with her man. A big fight erupted and I'm stuck in the middle trying to sort things out. I couldn't believe it. Things eventually calmed down and order was restored. I tried to explain to the locals that the guys were just up on holiday and didn't want trouble. Next thing the police showed up, at which point I thought we were all screwed. I went out and spoke to the coppers and told them the locals had started it and it had flared up out of nothing.

'Well, we don't take kindly to this sort of behaviour in our town.' They let us off with a slap on the wrists, which was just as well because Big Joe was in his bed and if he'd been knocked up to bail guys out of the nick he would have gone berserk. I'm sure our only saving grace was my Scottish accent. Had it been one of the English lads doing the talking we would have been for the high jump.

I received an injury to my foot whilst on that little tour and Joe and his assistant Jimmy Lumsden took me to Celtic Park for some treatment, where I met Mick McCarthy who was with them at the time. Mick was a sound guy. I found the pre-season training really tough that summer. I'd let myself slip a bit and getting that fitness and sharpness primed and back to its best was a bloody nightmare, but it paid off in the end.

I had another setback when my nose was accidentally broken by one of our own players during a training stint. It was a cracker, right over my face. The guy who did it was Glenn Humphreys and we'd had a bit of an argument and had nearly come to blows in the dressing room a few weeks earlier. We were having tea after training and I went to pick up this cup at the same time as he did. We were both naked (I can categorically state it was purely professional!) and for some daft reason he threw the hot tea all over me. Thankfully, it wasn't boiling! It sparked off a major rammy and we were very nearly boxing.

'See you,' I said to him, 'you're fuckin' mad!' He was a big lad but there's no way I was backing down. Joe heard all the commotion and stormed through then told both of us to get into his office. I said to Humphs, 'Let me do the talking, it was an accident OK?' We walked into the office and Joe asked, 'Right, what the hell's going on in there?'

'Well Joe, we both went to pick up the cup at the same time and Humphs got there first and accidentally spilled it over me. I just got a little burnt that's all.' I think he knew what the story was but bought it anyway.

'Right, no more of that nonsense in the dressing room. Get out the pair of you!'

The funny thing was big Humphs was a mate and we laughed about it later. Then he broke my nose in training which was great! We'd been having a bounce game seven-a-side and I flicked the ball past him, but he was an awful player for having his elbows out. He caught me a belter and put it well out. We had a new physio, Buster Footman, who was on his first day of duty at the club. What a start for him!

Buster turned out to be a great character. He had a really nice manner and was always having a laugh and a bit of banter with the lads. He was an ex-Royal Marine and, as you would expect, he was as tough as old boots. He became a legendary figure at City and must have held the unofficial title for the 'hardest man in England' due to his infamous dress code. Whether it was minus twenty degrees, howling with sleet, rain or snow, there he was decked out in a vest or T-shirt. He was definitely mental!

I was sent up to this private hospital, but they sent me back and said they couldn't do anything until the bruising went down. I went in to see the gaffer and said, 'Joe, I can't go about like this for three or four days! Can't you do something?' I then went to Bristol Royal Infirmary, who couldn't do nothing with it either, but the surgeon told me if I could get up to the private hospital in Clifton he would straighten it that afternoon. A new drug was being pioneered at the time which could anaesthetise you then bring you round after the operation without the usual long recovery period, so that's what I had.

That was me going to be out of action for three weeks so

Joe asked what I wanted to do. I told him I was going to go up to Scotland so I drove to Heathrow (there were no Bristol flights home in those days) and boarded a plane there. I wasn't a pretty sight, what with a bloody great stookie (plaster) on my nose and my face all swollen. I looked like I'd come off worst in a fifteen-rounder against Larry Holmes. This was the second occasion I'd had to fly looking like a body double for the Elephant Man. The plane wasn't very busy and when the stewardess approached she did a double take before asking if I'd like a drink.

'I'll have a Bacardi and coke please.'

She brought two of the miniature bottles back, which I scoffed in ten minutes. I stopped her again and asked if I could have another drink. This time she came back with four bottles and I downed them before we landed. I was a wee bit tipsy when I got off but it was a damn good flight!

Going back to Bristol played havoc with my emotions. I found it extremely difficult to leave my son Bradley and go back down, but there was nothing else I could do. I tried to focus on regaining my fitness again and getting back into the team. When I did return I began to hit some good form and helped myself to a few cracking goals. This purple patch hadn't gone unnoticed and as the months progressed I found out that a Scottish Premier Division team was having me watched.

I'd been on the phone to my ex-United team mate Doddsy who was now playing with our old 'New Firm' rivals Aberdeen, having spent only a few months in Switzerland with Neuchatel Xamax. He told me that representatives from the Dons had been down twice. I already knew because I'd spotted their manager Alex Smith. I reckoned if I kept playing well it might only be a matter of time before I was off and back up north.

I loved Bristol dearly and had settled in well, but going to Aberdeen would have meant I'd be a lot closer to my son.

We had a player who'd joined City, a Scot called Scott McGarvey whom I knew from the Under-21s. He was a bit of a wide guy, a Jack the Lad type, but we really hit it off and we used to have some great banter in the dressing room. He'd played for Man United in the early 80s and did reasonably well there. Anyway, we'd finish training and go up to the lounge for a bite to eat and some juice and I'd end up on the piano. With all this hush-hush Aberdeen activity going on I'd break into a chorus of 'The Northern Lights of Old Aberdeen' which usually coincided with Big Joe walking through the door. Scotty would be pissing himself laughing while Joe would just give me a look as if to say, 'are you takin' the piss?' He never did mention anything though.

Aberdeen had tabled two bids which were rejected by City. I'd been playing well and scored a screamer in the League Cup against Division One opponents Oxford United whom we beat 4-2. I followed that in the next round with two against Crystal Palace, whom we destroyed 4-1. (The team actually got as far as the semis where they narrowly lost out 2-1 over two legs to eventual winners Nottingham Forest). My goals, however, didn't go down too well with a certain person connected with Aberdeen. He contacted me on the phone and said, 'For fuck's sake Ralph, will you stop scoring goals? Every time you bang one in Joe's raising the fee by £10,000!'

The month was November and the year was 1988. My world was about to be turned upside down in an unimaginable way. Joe pulled me into his office on a Thursday morning after training for a 'chat'. From the beginning of that week I just felt something was going down, I could sense it. I closed the door behind me and waited to hear what the boss had to say. He didn't hang about and opened with the statement, 'There is *nobody* leaving this club!' He paused then continued, 'But in your circumstances I'm prepared to make an exception.' At that moment I thought it was because we'd split up and my wife had gone back to Scotland. Immediately, I said to myself, 'That's it; I'm off to Aberdeen then.'

Joe broke my temporary thought process and said, 'I've accepted an offer for you, but it's not at Aberdeen.' Again, he had me thinking then panicking, 'Oh no, it could be anywhere, it could be fuckin' Scunthorpe or something!' His next words hit me like a demolition ball in the kisser, 'It's Man United.'

'Fuck off Joe! Are you winding me up?'

'No, you've got to speak to Fergie now.'

I said, 'Well you'd better get him on the phone then.' It was bang on twelve o'clock.

'All right son?' he asked.

'Yeah, fine.'

'You're playing well now.'

'Er, well yeah, I'm a bit fitter now.'

'What do you think then? Do you fancy it?'

'Well, I can't really say no to you can I?'

'Right,' he said, 'come straight into the ground. I've got to go to a dinner tonight. I'll wait here for you.'

I put the phone down and stood there utterly shell-shocked. Joe smiled and wished me all the best. My head was spinning. One minute I was going to Aberdeen (so I thought), next thing I'm on my way to meet Alex Ferguson and finalise a deal that would take me to Man United! As Greavsie used to say on the TV show *Saint and Greavsie*, 'It's a funny old game!' It was just mental.

Before I shot up to Manchester I had a dilemma to sort out in Bristol. Prior to the transfer speculation I had begun looking for a house. Things were going nicely on the park and off it. I'd adjusted positively to my break-up and settled in well to the West Country life. I put a £100 deposit on a house, a new-build in a town called Nailsea which lies around seven miles to the south west of Bristol. One of the players was with me at the time and told me another team mate Stevie Galliers was selling his house so I drove a couple of hundred yards up the road to view it. It was a bigger place for the same price so I said to Galls I'd buy it from him. The deal was meant to go through on the Friday but, due to complications with his solicitor, it stalled. Galls told me to just move my stuff in anyway. My mate Gerry who'd just split up with his wife was supposed to be moving in with me as well while he got things sorted out. The following Thursday, the same day I'd received the news about Man United, my furniture was being unloaded off the van and into the house. I drew up in my car and said to Gerry, 'What am I going to do? I've just been sold.'

'You're fuckin' joking,' he said. 'Who is it? Aberdeen?'

'No, it's Man United.' He was as shocked as I had been. I told him just to move in till we got something else arranged. I phoned Stevie Galliers that night and explained the situation and that I wasn't going ahead with the deal. I offered to rent it from him in the short term but he asked me to remove my gear from his premises. It took about two weeks to get it cleared back out. Stevie wasn't too impressed with all this and never spoke to me again. I think he felt I should still have gone ahead with the purchase, but there was nothing I could do. It was all Man United's fault . . . but I wasn't complaining.

12

DREAM MOVE TO MAN UNITED

As I drove up to Manchester my mind was a myriad of contrasting emotions. Adrenaline pumped through my body with a mixture of joyful elation, trepidation, apprehension, fear and excitement, the latter definitely at the top of the pile. To say I was buzzing would be a gross understatement. I gazed out of the car window and told myself 'life is good'. There was of course the small element of fear, the going into the unknown. It wouldn't be right not to experience *some* fear – we are talking *Manchester United* after all!

A million questions raced through my head, but hardly any were answered. One thing I was sure of, however, was that I wouldn't be overwhelmed just because of who they were. I was always confident in my own ability, always. I actually relished the thought of meeting Alex Ferguson and hearing what his plans were and just where I figured in them.

It was in fact only quite recently that I found out how the whole Man United interest had come about, after talking to the person mainly responsible for igniting the spark in Fergie's mind. Archie Knox (who was Fergie's assistant) said to him, 'What about Ralph Milne? He's maybe not as electric pace-wise as he was, but he could still do a job.' Subsequently, the club had me watched and must have liked what they saw. For a team whose history speaks for itself, the odd FA Cup success was scant consolation for the Red Mancunian masses, who demanded a League Championship. Not since 1967 had the old trophy graced the Old Trafford cabinet.

Enter Fergie in November 1986 to turn the club's fortunes around, or so they hoped. He had been lured away from Aberdeen after a hugely successful period there where he won all the domestic honours and an historic European Cup Winners' Cup trophy. His predecessor at United, Big Ron Atkinson, had bags of charisma and character and was popular with the players but only had two FA Cup wins to show for five seasons' work. There was no League Championship and that was unacceptable. Big Ron's reign had left a bevvy-culture legacy amongst some players, which Fergie had a lot of trouble undoing. This wasn't an ideal situation, given my own liking for the odd beer or two.

I reached the Thelwall Viaduct at Warrington and joined a massive traffic jam. I still had about twenty miles to go and was beginning to panic. I couldn't let Fergie down for this all-important first meeting – it was unthinkable. It was after five when I finally reached Old Trafford and Alex Ferguson was waiting. His dinner was scheduled for 7.30pm, so things were a little tight to say the least.

'C'mon,' he said, 'you'll have to come with me to the house, I need to be ready and out.'

My jaw hit the deck at the sight of his house – it was awesome! When we entered I couldn't help but stare at the magnificent surroundings in which I found myself. It wasn't over-the-top lavish grandeur, just a quality which most of us can only dream about. It oozed class and all of it earned by the blood, sweat and tears of honest hard graft for which he is renowned. His OBE award hung proudly on a wall and a snooker room lay off to the side. He took me into his lounge and my head was trying its best to mimic the young girl's head in the film *The Exorcist* and swivel in a complete 360 degree arc. I couldn't stop gazing at all the photos and memorabilia. I sat down in a trance-like state and tried to concentrate on what he was saying, but it was useless. Was I awestruck? Absolutely, completely and most definitely!

He began, 'OK, here's what I'm gonna do for you . . . blah, blah, blah.' The words went in one ear and straight out the other without registering. He would have been better talking to the other chair; he might have got a little more reaction from it than I was giving out. The hypnotic state tailed off just in time to hear him say, 'Is that OK with you then?' I'm sure he must have noticed my rather wandered condition as he awaited my reply. I looked for a pen and piece of paper to sign (which weren't there). He could've put a document down in front of me saying I was solely responsible for the *Titanic* sinking and I would have signed it!

Fergie informed me he was going to sell the Dane Jesper Olsen and that my left foot was better than Wee Strachan's (Gordon), which it probably was. Therefore the role he wanted me to fill was as a left winger. I didn't have a problem with that. I'd trained my left as a young lad and reaped the benefits as I'd matured. Switching wings didn't faze me at all. In an ideal world I would have preferred the right and been more at home but I didn't have a choice and in all honesty I would have played in the goal if Fergie had asked me, anything just to pull on that Red jersey.

I'd already missed the signing deadline of 5pm for inclusion in Saturday's squad but I don't think I would have been thrown in so soon anyway, even if I had made it. The manager said he'd now wait until the Monday to do it. He offered me to stay in his house that night or I could go to a hotel. I opted for the latter, which turned out to be the luxurious Crown Plaza Holiday Inn. The Northern Ireland internationalist Mal Donaghy was staying there, having recently been signed from Luton Town for £650,000. I thought it would be a bit off staying at the manager's house but it shows the kind of man Alex Ferguson was to even make an offer like that. The other thing that swayed my decision in favour of the hotel was a cool pint of lager. Well, I had to celebrate somehow!

I was that elated at what had just happened. To be honest, the whole day had been very surreal, my head was in the clouds. All I kept asking myself was, 'Is this for real?' Once I got to the hotel, though, my thoughts switched to a more negative mode and I reasoned with myself that if Fergie had *really* wanted me, he would have taken my signature right there and then no matter what. In reality, this was absurd but it undoubtedly occupied my mind for a period that night.

On the Friday morning I walked into the dressing room at the Cliff training ground and I spotted wee Gordon Strachan who looked up at me, looked down and then looked back up again. His surprise was obvious. 'Fuckin' hell, what are *you* doing here?' he asked.

'What does it look like?' I shot back. Someone then shouted over, 'There's your peg there Ralph.' It had recently been vacated by Kevin Moran who had gone to Blackburn Rovers and was stuck slap-bang right in the middle of Norman Whiteside and Paul McGrath. Much has been documented already about the heavy drinking culture which prevailed throughout the Big Ron Atkinson years, something which Alex Ferguson was trying desperately hard to eradicate. It was a habit which he didn't enjoy and pinpointed as one of the main reasons the team had been consistently under-achieving.

When he took over at Man U in 1986, Fergie inherited a squad which included a whole host of international stars who were not producing the goods on the park and who were, he felt, unacceptably lacking in proper fitness. Top players like Whiteside, McGrath and Bryan Robson were well known for enjoying a good bevvy session as were some of the others. It's no secret that I enjoyed a good session myself and I knew I would end up getting involved with them sooner rather than later.

My new peg neighbours were of course two of the heroes of the United faithful. Big Norm (Whiteside) had come through the youth ranks and was a bustling, no nonsense, rough type of player who also possessed a good touch. His fiery temper and aggressive style often had him at loggerheads with opposition players and referees alike. He was still fairly young but had already played in two World Cups for Northern Ireland and still holds the record for being the youngest ever player to appear in the 1982 World Cup finals at the raw age of seventeen. He suffered badly from problems with a knee injury which had a detrimental effect on his first team appearances. Big McGrath was a strong but skilful defender who, like Norman, also suffered problems with his knees. He too was an internationalist, but he played for the Republic of Ireland and it wasn't long before I got familiar with their friendly rivalry and banter over playing for the two Irish sides. I felt like a dwarf at times, stuck in between these two giants.

Back to that Friday morning and my first day there. I trained with the squad and was put through my paces. Archie Knox took the session and I really enjoyed it. I think it was because it was the good old-fashioned Scottish type of training, much the same as I'd experienced with Wee Jim and Wattie Smith. This was something which I'd really missed at Charlton. Afterwards Fergie told me to come back to Old Trafford – he was going to sign me right there and then without delay. He took me up to the boardroom and I signed the contract which was for eighteen months, terrific I thought. The fee was £170,000. This also included a club car and I was given the choice of a Ford Escort XR3i Cabriolet (which had been Jesper Olsen's wife's – he had a great big Jag!) or a Ford Escort RS Turbo – in my opinion, two of the worst cars you can imagine. I didn't want either of them. At the time I owned a cracking Audi. In the end I took the RS Turbo which went like shit off a shovel!

My old club Charlton had a sell-on clause in the contract when I signed for Bristol and they ended up with around forty grand in their pockets from my United deal. I thought when I'd signed my Man U contract that was that and I'd just head back to the hotel. However, I was taken to their press room which back then wasn't nearly as plush as it is now but was still damned impressive. About twenty reporters from the press greeted my entrance into the room. I couldn't believe it. Some of the questions I was being asked were just plain daft. They made a big issue of the transfer fee, indicating that it wasn't a huge amount. For a club such as Manchester United it was peanuts really. They (the press) latched right onto this and were saying things like, 'And where has he come from – a Third Division club?' It felt quite belittling, sitting there listening to that. They were putting me down before I'd even kicked a ball. Some papers later printed that the fee was £175,000 but if that was the case then five grand must have gone missing. In the end it was a simple misquote.

My first ever appearance in the famous red jersey was a reserve match against Coventry City. Unfortunately the game only lasted about thirty minutes and was abandoned due to thick fog. My next game was again for the reserves, but this time it was at Old Trafford. I don't remember who it was against but I do remember scoring an absolute peach. I cracked it from outside the box and it went right in the top corner. When I came off at the end Fergie said, 'Great goal son, great goal. You'll be playing Saturday.'

On Saturday, 19 November 1988 I ran out onto the turf at the famous Old Trafford stadium for my first team debut against Southampton. It was a huge buzz and just a little bit different from what I'd been used to at Bristol, with somewhere in the region of 40,000 fans creating a brilliant atmosphere. This was the big stage now and it felt very special. I'm sure the fans must have been asking themselves, 'What can we expect from this Scottish guy who's come from a Third Division outfit?' For any player who pulls on that red shirt for Manchester United, the fans' expectations are always going to be exceedingly high. It is the kind of pressure that goes naturally with the job of playing for one of the most famous clubs in the world. The adrenaline was pumping big time as I awaited the ref's whistle to start the match but it was more in anticipation than fear. I certainly didn't feel out of my depth; after all, I'd played against some of the biggest names in European football and occasionally destroyed them.

At the end of what can only be described as a 'shite' ninety minutes of football, we walked off the pitch, very grateful to have earned a 2-2 draw. Much of this was down to the industrious efforts of our captain Bryan Robson who at times seemed to be operating everywhere at once. To put it bluntly, we were dire. The game itself largely passed me by and I never saw much of the ball. During the match our keeper Big Jazzer (Jim Leighton) had a calamitous moment when one of the Southampton players launched a huge up-and-under from around the halfway line, which he fumbled and basically chucked into the back of our net. I couldn't believe it. I was saying, 'Fuck sake Jazzer, not on my debut!' Luckily, goals from Sparky (Mark Hughes) and Robbo (Bryan Robson) salvaged the point.

When I joined Man U the team's form had been mainly inconsistent since the start of the season. This must have been agonisingly frustrating for Fergie given the previous season's positive finish of runners-up to bitter rivals Liverpool. There's no doubting he'd be wishing to go one better this season but it wasn't looking too clever at this early stage. Sadly, we were denied all the magic that European football brings due to the on-going ban following the Heysel Stadium disaster.

My first goal for the club came against none other than my former employers Charlton Athletic in a match we won 3-0. The ball came over from a corner which I caught sweetly and volleyed from the edge of the box. It was already going in but took a wee deflection. I wasn't caring, it was *my* goal, my first *Manchester United* goal and I was over the moon! Before it, the Charlton fans had been dishing it out to me with some heavy stick and singing, 'He's fat, he's round, he's bouncing on the ground' which I found quite amusing because I was in fairly good shape at the time. You can't beat a goal to clamp the mouths of opposition fans. I remember playing well throughout that game and, after it, Fergie said to me if it hadn't been for my runs we may have struggled a bit.

We then slumped to two away defeats at Coventry and Arsenal before facing Brian Clough's high-flying Nottingham Forest team on Boxing Day at Old Trafford. We trained on the Christmas Day but I never received an invite from any of the players to have dinner with them so I jumped in the car and drove down to Bristol to spend the rest of the day with my girlfriend Lee. I made sure I didn't overdo it with the drink and went to bed at nine. All the players had to be back at the ground for a pre-match meal at midday so I left sharp that morning to avoid any possible roadworks or delays.

Cloughie had been slowly rebuilding his Forest side after the heady days of the late 70s and early 80s when they had won major honours including two European Cups. His present squad included rising stars such as Neil Webb, Des Walker, Stuart Pearce and his son Nigel Clough. We managed to give the fans a late Christmas present with a 2-0 victory. Sparky scored the first then I got the second from a simple tap-in after their keeper had blocked a shot, again from Sparky.

Then came what many, if not all United fans, regard as *the* game of the season – the encounter with Liverpool. The respective cities are separated by a mere thirty-odd miles, but the rivalry both on and off the field is intense. Man U had been forced to live in the shadows of their Scouse neighbours and watch helplessly as Championships and European and domestic cups piled up in the Anfield trophy cabinet. This was a bitter pill to swallow for all connected with the club. United had already lost the first battle by a goal to nil away in what was only the second match of the campaign. Now they were desperate for revenge and I had the opportunity to help the cause. It was New Years Day 1989 and I was about to experience all the tribalism, passion, fanaticism and fierce rivalry for which this tie is so famously known. The gaffer had celebrated his forty-seventh birthday only twenty-four hours earlier and we wanted to give him (and the fans) a great victory to celebrate. We owed it to them after some poor performances previously.

Old Trafford was a cauldron of noise as around 45,000 voices shook the ground to its foundations. The atmosphere was electric. I remember winning a tackle against Steve McMahon, who had a reputation for being a bit of a hard man, and leaving him trailing in my wake. I just thought, 'Fuck you mate, I'll see you later!' With the scores locked at 0-0 the game exploded into life with around twenty minutes remaining when John Barnes cut inside our box and sent the ball over big Jazzer and into the net. Their fans hardly had time to celebrate though as a minute later we were right back in it when fellow Scot Brian McClair scored a spectacular volley. The crowd went absolutely nuts.

It got even crazier four minutes later when we took the lead through a great Mark Hughes strike. If our fans were in delirium with *that* goal, Russell Beardsmore sent them into ecstatic pandemonium shortly afterwards with a third and decisive goal. The ground was bouncing! 3-1 it finished and we were in Red heaven. I genuinely believe I could have picked up the Man Of The Match award after that particular game, I felt my display warranted it. That was probably my best game for United.

There was no time for celebrations after it though, as we

had to get straight on the coach and travel to Middlesbrough for a game the following day which was scheduled to kick off at 12.00pm. If I remember correctly they hadn't played on New Years Day so were fit, fresh and ready to take us on. The euphoria of our exploits against Liverpool was soon forgotten and we were brought crashing back down to earth with a massive bang and a 1-0 defeat.

Our next League game was against shock troops Millwall who were going great guns at the time. I ran them ragged that day and had a really good game, supplying the cross for Tony Gill who hammered in a terrific volley. We crushed them 3-0. (Poor Tony was to suffer a horrendous leg break just a couple of months later in a match with Nottingham Forest which ended his career.) Around this time Clayton Blackmore and I were chosen to join an all-star select to play in a benefit match for Mick Baxter of Preston North End, who had his life tragically cut short through cancer. It was a very emotional day and players such as Kenny Dalglish, Trevor Steven and Frank Worthington turned out to play.

A week before our mauling of Millwall, the FA Cup began, which was probably our only realistic hope of silverware that season, having been knocked out of the Littlewoods (League) Cup just before I arrived. Our form in the League was erratic and inconsistent and not that of Championship-Winning material. I'm not sure of the reasons why but Man United always seem to have had a great love affair with the FA Cup. I think they, more than any other team, embody the whole spirit, drama and passion that go with that competition.

We took three laboured efforts to finally overcome our Third Round opponents QPR then brushed Oxford United aside with a 4-0 rout in the next round. We drew Bournemouth away in the fifth and were extremely lucky to come away with a 1-1 draw. Sparky scored the goal and gave us the lifeline for a replay. (Luther Blissett was playing for them at the time and was another guy whom I would come into contact with some years later.) Over 50,000 fans packed into Old Trafford for that game, which gives some indication of just how special the FA Cup is to them. Brian McClair saved our blushes and bagged the only goal of the game. As the quarter-finals approached the excitement began to grow and thoughts wandered to the possibility of playing at Wembley in an FA Cup final. It wasn't to be though as Nottingham Forest dumped us out of the tournament with a 1-0 win, much to the disappointment of ourselves and Fergie and possibly even more so to the vast majority of the 55,000 fans who turned up to cheer us on.

During the Cup run our League form had been good initially but a defeat and a draw prior to the quarter-finals stalled our little winning streak. A week later we got back to business and I scored my third goal of the season in a 2-0 win over Luton Town. From then on in though our form dipped dramatically and we finished in a very poor position of eleventh in the League. There was one positive outcome at the end of that season, Sparky Hughes' return to United had seen him put in some great performances and he was quite rightly awarded the PFA Player Of The Year.

That Fergie was under pressure from both the fans and the board was all too noticeable. He knew the blend wasn't right. There was massive pressure on him, but he was the kind of man who absorbed it himself and didn't lay blame on his players. That took a lot of heart and courage. I think we as players knew only too well ourselves that things weren't right on the park either and the team weren't operating as a solid, functioning unit. With the calibre of players at the club we should have been up there challenging with the best of them, but it just wasn't happening.

I still believe passionately that I had a right to be part of the Manchester United set-up – some fans may disagree, but they're entitled to their opinions. Something which had given me a real feeling of satisfaction were the few words which I received from the boss himself. He'd praised me for encouraging and supporting young Lee Sharpe on the park. I think he was only seventeen and had forced his way into the team on merit to play at left back. He had an obvious talent and could motor as well. I would always try and get back to cover him and talk to him, that kind of thing, and it was good to see how his career progressed.

I had been at the club for seven months now and knew that Fergie would be looking to bring some fresh faces in to strengthen the squad. A big part of me felt that my chance had maybe gone. With eleven months of my contract still left to run all I could do was keep plugging away and trying my best.

13

A DAY AT THE RACES

My eyes were certainly opened during that first season at Man United. I was aware of the drink culture which existed at the club and I freely admit I became involved in it whole-heartedly. Before I arrived there some of the players told me about the infamous 'Sharp Suite' and the drinking sessions that went on there. Sharp were of course the club's sponsors at the time. When guys were out injured they would head up there and get tore into the champagne, which I'm told aided recovery! This was probably one of the first things Fergie had knocked on the head when he arrived. It must have been daunting for him confronting some of the biggest names in British football to lay down the law and tell them that things were changing. They were, but very slowly. The club captain, Robbo (Bryan Robson), had a huge influence at Manchester United, especially among the players, and I suppose there was a bit of a battle of wills going on since Fergie's arrival from Aberdeen.

My fitness was good that season but my team mates McGrath and Whiteside were, more often than not, struggling with injuries. I would finish training and have my bath or shower then I'd sit down with the pair of them. 'Norman,' I'd say, 'are we going for lunch?'

'What does the Big Man say?' he'd reply. I'd turn to Paul and say, 'Big Man, are we going for lunch?'

'What does Norman say?'

'Norman says yes.'

'That's it then, we're going for lunch,' he'd confirm and off we'd go straight out on the bevvy. I'll tell you what, these boys could drink! It wasn't wild but they certainly were *heavy* sessions. Thankfully, I was still able to go out and train the next day. Sometimes the pair of them would wind me up and Norm would start at Paul with, 'You ya big fuckin' black, Fenian bastard!' Big McGrath would hit back, 'Ya dirty Proddy, Orange bastard!' I'd be shitting myself waiting for the Clash Of The Titans to kick off but they'd laugh and I'd realise the bastards were taking the piss.

Some of Paul's benders have gone down in club folklore but, of course, that's not how Fergie would view them. He had the unenviable task of trying to get the Big Man to change his ways and get back on the straight and narrow. Now I'm no angel myself, but there were times when he was still half-cut and turning up to train. The injury situation only made matters worse and with Big Norm also out it was all too tempting to pass the day away with a pint or two, or ten. Fergie must have been banging his head off the wall with some of the top stars' unwillingness to ditch the drink.

Both my big mates were unbelievable players when fit and on their game but the on-going path of self-destruction coupled with constant injuries meant the writing was on the wall. One time we were waiting outside on Paul after he'd been pulled in to the office. He was told a specialist would be coming in to give his knees a proper going over and if he found them to be knackered then, basically, his career was over. I said to Paul, 'They can't do that. The first thing you need to do is get on the phone to Gordon Taylor at the PFA and explain the situation.'

Paul was famously offered a retirement package from the club but turned it down. I remember an episode when he'd reported himself not fit but the physio told him to go out and have a jog. The physio then informed Alex Ferguson that he *was* fit so Fergie named him in his squad. The Big Man didn't know about his inclusion and went on a right bender. He turned up the next day in no fit state to play and Fergie went off his nut. I'm sure he was shouting at Sir Bobby Charlton saying, 'See, he doesn't want to play, he doesn't even want to be a fuckin' sub!' I personally had a lot of time for Paul. This was maybe due to the similarities in our characters. He was a big gentle giant whom I rated as a top class bloke.

Socialising with the rest of the boys wasn't easy though as most of them stayed on the south side of Manchester in the Cheshire area. They were also in a different league from me wages-wise and this reflected in their houses and lifestyles. Realistically, I couldn't compete and when my time was up in the hotel I had to look for something a little smaller. Fergie was brilliant with me when I began looking for a house. The usual time limit of three months was up but a wee phone call from the boss to the Chairman Martin Edwards secured an extension of a month while I waited on the house which I'd purchased to be completed.

Originally I'd looked at a fairly modest mid-terraced house down in Cheshire priced at eighty grand but a new housing development to the north of the city in Prestwich was offering a new-build for £79,000. I didn't even have to think about it and put the deposit down. The other good thing was it was situated near to the training ground.

It was funny when Mal (Donaghy) and I were nearing the end of our stay in the hotel and Fergie said to us, 'You boys will be out of there soon eh? Remember and pay your phone bills.' Now, I had never put any drinks on my tab but Mal wasn't caring. He'd also been making plenty of calls back to Northern Ireland. He nearly shit a brick when Fergie had said that but he was winding us up big time, which was just as well! Mr Ferguson did possess a great sense of humour at times.

When I moved into my new home it was something of a relief to get back to normality although the hotel was an absolute cracker. Lee, who had been commuting back and forth from Bristol when she could, moved in straight away. Thinking back I don't know why the hell I'd bought a house with four bedrooms when there was only the two of us. Once I had a permanent base I was able to travel back to Dundee more often and see my son and also bring my parents down for wee breaks. I recall one time when five or six of the Man U lads came up to my neck of the woods for a beer and a bit of banter before heading home, which I thought was a nice touch from them.

My love of gambling and a punt on the horses together with a 'beer and a bit of banter' landed a few of us in hot water when we decided to have a day at the races and take in the Cheltenham Gold Cup. This was on the Thursday, just two days before our crucial FA Cup quarter-final tie against Nottingham Forest at Old Trafford. Robbo, his mate 'Blackie', Steve Bruce and I had planned to travel down after we finished training that morning and enjoy the festivities at one of Britain's best-loved events on the racing calendar. Robbo was banned from driving at the time but had arranged for his chauffeur to do the business and take us there and back.

We arrived nice and sharp at the university football pitches for training and I was well prepared with essential items such as suit, hat and washbag. The wind was knocked from our sails though when a staff member approached and said, 'The manager's in a meeting just now and won't be taking the training till later on.' We could really have done without this news as we wanted to be there for the first race at 2.15pm. On hearing this Robbo took the real hump. We were all like, 'Fuck me, what's going on here?' Fergie eventually turned up about 10.30am and told us we'd start training at 11.00am. By now Robbo was fuming!

We started the warm-up, jogging up and down the pitch and Fergie shouts over, 'Hey Robbo, are you thinking of going to Cheltenham this week?' He always seemed to be one step ahead of the game. I think he'd twigged straight away and was deliberately trying to prevent us from going with stalling tactics. Robbo answered back, 'Well yeah, I was actually.'

'When were you thinking on going?'

'Today.'

Fergie's voice was raised a notch or two and a hint of anger laced his words. 'Going to fuckin' Cheltenham *today*? You're going all the way down there and back, cramped up in a car and we've got a big game on Saturday? You're not fuckin' going!' There was a brief period of silence and we all carried on jogging. Fergie then piped up again, 'Anybody else thinking on going?'

'Yeah, me.' It was Stevie Bruce. I thought, 'I'm not fuckin' believing this!' Brucie had just made a proper *James Hunt* of it by coming clean. Fergie shouts back, 'You? You don't know the back end of a horse from the front! You're not going either!' I kept my mouth shut. He must have had a wee think about the situation then said, 'Right, if you're going to Cheltenham be it on your own head! You can go if you go in a helicopter,' he conceded. Robbo argued back that he'd need landing times and clearance etc. Again, Fergie just said, 'Be it on your head.'

What you have to remember at that time is Fergie was under increasing pressure to produce results for the club and with the sway Robbo held, he probably felt he needed to give his captain some slack. The one thing Robbo had in his favour was that when he was fit and playing he seemed to inspire all around him and sometimes he was capable of single-handedly turning a match. His will to win was incredible. The club needed him, Fergie needed him and we all knew it.

When training was finished I went straight into the shower, got washed, shaved, suited up, hat on and was out in a flash, looking the business I may add. Robbo's chauffeur was waiting outside with Blackie so I jumped into the motor and joined them, followed closely by Robbo himself. There was no sign of Brucie. We didn't have time to hang about so the driver stepped on the gas and shot off. We were desperate to get there for the first race. As we hammered along the M56 the phone went in the car – it was Brucie. 'Wait for me at Knutsford,' he said so we pulled in, well late by now. When he finally caught up he jumped in the back with me and Blackie. Someone asked him what had happened. He explained, 'Well I went up to see him (Fergie) and told him I'd be much more relaxed watching a day's racing than being at home with my wife and kids.' Fergie then basically chucked him out of his office. Brucie took a few moments to settle himself then slowly turned to me with an accusing kind of stare and said, 'You're some c*** you are!'

'What are you on about?' I threw back.

'Well *you* never said anything (at training)!'

I replied, 'See if *you* hadn't said anything, we'd be twenty minutes further down the fuckin' road you daft c***!'

We got there for ten-past two after a white-knuckle ride on the motorway. All the way down I had been studying form in the paper and had picked out the favourite for the first race. I told the rest of them to get their dough on it – it was a cert! We'd managed to get ourselves into a fairly exclusive area and wasted no time in ordering up the champagne. We had it sussed and took it in turns to order more drinks and hold the table while everyone else went out to bet on the races.

I had £400 on my first horse, Forest Sun, and that beautiful specimen of power and athleticism stormed home at 7-4. Three hundred pounds up already and the champers was going down a treat. We had an unbelievable day with everybody winning and we ended up back at the Four Seasons hotel just outside Manchester airport. We were in company and the focus turned to some card game which I'd never seen or played in my life. Someone took about four hundred quid from me, I was so pissed I didn't know what I was doing.

There were no repercussions from Fergie or the club the following day and it was back to business as usual. It's just a pity we never produced the same form as some of our horses when we played Forest in the cup. Those who witnessed our performance might rightfully say we played like cart-horses.

14

SUMMER OF 89

I was hoping like hell I'd be included in Manchester United's pre-season tour of Thailand and Japan during the summer of 1989. Ten years previously, when I was with Dundee United, I'd missed out on the opportunity of going to Japan for a tournament due to some 'other business' which I had to attend. Even if I hadn't been involved in this 'other business' I still wouldn't have been going to Japan according to my then manager Jim McLean. He pulled me into his office prior to the trip and told me, using a colourful variety of creative language, that I wasn't going and that 'Boney' (John Reilly) was in front of me in the pecking order. (John ended up being left at home under mysterious circumstances after being cruelly informed he wasn't going, only two days before the squad were due to travel!) I let him finish his rant then said simply, 'I know.'

'What do you fuckin' mean you know?'

'Because I'm going to Austria,' I replied.

'What do you mean you're going to Austria?' he barked.

'I'm in the Scottish Youth team.' He went bananas and threatened to have me removed from that squad as well. I can't remember what I'd done to upset him in such a way for him to act like that. I think he possibly wanted me to stay in Dundee that summer and pick berries or something. Well I *did* go to Austria. Meanwhile, out in Japan, he was sending Hamish the goalie home over a disagreement of two yards!

I thought back over the last few months of the season and how it had nose-dived and I knew Fergie would be looking to strengthen the squad. I was unsure if I would remain in his plans for the coming season. Mike Phelan arrived from Norwich City for £750,000, as did Neil Webb from Nottingham Forest for a whopping £1.5 million! Two United players then headed in the opposite direction and out the door. It was my buddies McGrath and Whiteside. Fergie's patience had obviously run out, what with the bevvying antics and time off the job due to frequent injuries.

Big Norm was first to go in a move to the Blue half of Merseyside when he joined Everton. Big Paul received his news in what would be described as more unorthodox circumstances. A load of us were at a barbeque at Robbo's house all having a great time, especially the Big Man – he was blootered! Some of us were in the back garden playing pool when Robbo's wife shouted to him, 'That's the manager on the phone.' He clearly knew where we'd be as his spies were more adept than a team of crack KGB agents. Robbo took the phone then shouted, 'Paul, he wants *you*.' As he spoke to Fergie on the phone I tried to discreetly stretch my ear over to hear what was being said. When he put it down I asked, 'Hey Big Man, what was all that about then?'

'He's just sold me!'

'What do you mean he's just sold you?'

'He's just sold me to Aston Villa.'

'Aren't you getting a say in the matter?'

'No. He says I'm out the door.' The double sale of those two, who were big favourites among the fans, undoubtedly served as a clear indication of how Alex Ferguson intended to change things for the good of Man United. It may not have been popular with the masses but Fergie didn't take the job on looking for Brownie points from anyone. Slowly but surely he was forcing his will and trying his damnedest to erase that hard-drinking legacy. However, those among us who liked a little sherry or two weren't quite ready to go teetotal – not just yet anyway!

When the list of names went up for the trip to Thailand and Japan I could have run through the streets of Salford bollock-naked singing 'I'm So Excited' by The Pointer Sisters (well maybe just the chorus! My name was on it and I was going!). Before we left, us players had a bit of a contentious issue with the club over daily money allowances. The club was offering a bare minimum, which was something like £14 a day for our soft drinks and water etc. Nobody was happy with that and we had a players' meeting to discuss this.

Robbo approached Fergie and said we wanted £500 and £50 phone call allowance per room. I couldn't believe what he was asking for but in the end nothing was resolved. We all met at Manchester airport about seven or eight in the morning to fly down to London. I'd been studying form with the horses so I turned to Robbo and said, 'See this horse, it's a fuckin' bricker!' I'm sure we went on the bunce (share) and put about four hundred quid on it between us. The problem was we'd be in the air when the race set off and wouldn't find out if we were quids in until we arrived in Bangkok.

Thankfully, though, Fergie eased our minds and also the

whole squad's when we got to London and he told us, 'Do what you want lads, it's a long journey.' He meant of course within reason but still, it was a great gesture and afforded us some quality chill time. We had about eleven hours to fill on the flight but, unfortunately, most of us had forgotten our chess sets and tiddlywinks counters. Luckily we had contingency plans all drawn up in case of such a disaster which basically involved going right on the piss! We did employ some recreation in the form of card 'schooleys' with big dough changing hands. Fergie (who was in another part of the plane with Archie) didn't seem to mind us having a bit of social fun, although no one was out of order.

The first thing that hit you when you landed was the incredible heat, it was stifling. I actually found it quite hard to breathe. The fact we were well bevvied didn't help matters much either. In the terminal we were greeted by hordes of 'fans', mostly Thai locals who'd got wind of our arrival and were anxious to see us. Fergie gave us half an hour to go and chat with them and sign autographs etc. In between I managed to make a swift phone call home to see how our horse had got on. Apparently it was still running even though the race had finished hours ago! Fantastic start to me and Robbo's tour! We boarded our coach and the banter and laughing soon died away. Our hotel destination was a horrendous journey through mental traffic and smog-filled skies and the drinking freedom we had enjoyed on the flight was now terminated. It was time to let the hangovers kick in and enjoy the tranquil scenery.

It was early afternoon (their time) when we arrived and Fergie ordered everyone to bed, which was fair enough as we were completely shattered. One thing which puzzled me was our luggage – it was already at the place and in our rooms!

It was kind of weird, I felt like some foreign diplomat. We could have had *anything* in those cases. Now I've pulled a few strokes in my time, but I certainly wouldn't go down that path and not in Thailand. I suppose this was something that was new and alien to me. Anyway, I was roomed up with Mal Donaghy so we settled in and grabbed some much needed shut-eye.

In the early evening we went downstairs and joined the others for a meal. It was around eight o'clock when the manager said, 'OK lads, you've got some free time. Senior players back for midnight, first team players back for 1 o'clock.' That was it, we were straight out on the town. We jumped in these little tuk-tuks which were like motorised go-carts and headed down to the infamous Patpong red-light district. Basically it consists of two parallel streets full of bars, adult entertainment and market stalls selling all the usual tourist junk. We had a few beers then made our way back to the hotel. Fergie was completely over the moon. The whole squad had made it back on time without any mishaps or incidents.

We were given the green light to carry on drinking at the hotel bar which we took full advantage of. One of the young lads spoiled it for himself though when he sneaked back out and was clocked by the club doctor. When the manager found out he ended up with a severe rap on the knuckles which hit him hard in the pocket. The next morning we assembled for training which was comical. Some of them hadn't even been to bed, it was just hopeless. To add to the calamitous situation the pitch was about as flat as a ploughed field, there were balls flying everywhere.

We spent three days there and played a match against the Thai national team and if I remember correctly we drew 1-1 with Robbo getting the goal. Their fans were unbelievably fanatical. I think a lot of it was to do with the instantly recognisable Man United logo and our whole presence of actually being in their country. I would imagine the opportunity doesn't present itself that often when they can watch a world famous football team play in their own backyard. It was a fabulous experience and the people were among some of the friendliest I've ever had the pleasure of meeting.

We left the claustrophobic hustle and bustle of Bangkok behind and flew to Japan for the second leg of our tour in which we were due to play their national side and Everton in a mini tournament. We were based in the massive port city of Kobe which was beautiful, though some five and a half years later the city was to suffer one of the worst recorded earthquakes in Japanese history. We played our first game against Everton and who was in their starting line-up? None other than Big Norman Whiteside who went on to score a brilliant twenty-five-yard volley! A few of us (and possibly even Fergie himself) were thinking at that moment, 'Is this the shape of things to come for the season ahead? Was Big Norm going to come back and haunt his former club?' I stayed on the subs bench for that match, which we lost 3-1.

The squad finished training one morning and were then told we could go shopping in the afternoon. 'Yeah right!' We did venture out and ended up in the famous Moto-machi area, which was like a massive arcade with streets that seemed to go on forever. Every couple of hundred yards another street would cross over at right angles. With the whole lot being under one roof it was undeniably impressive. We popped into a couple of shops but everything was ultra-expensive so that idea was quickly ditched. This was in the first stretch, which was called Moto-machi 1, with each crossroads going into the next Moto-machi and, knowing the Japanese, no doubt went into Moto-machi infinity! I was with Mark Hughes, Neil Webb and Clayton Blackmore and, as we wandered down to number two then three doing nothing but window-shopping, I stopped and said to the others, 'Fuck this, I am *sick* of this! I'm going for a beer.'

'Where are you going to get a beer *here*?' they asked.

'Licky's Bar,' I said.

'What do you mean *Licky's Bar*? Where the hell is that?'

'Wait a minute, you're playing for the biggest club in the world and you don't have any fuckin' vision?' I paused for a moment then said, 'It's back in Moto-machi 1!'

The boozer and the bookies – that's the first two things you suss out when wandering in an alien environment! Now that it had been mentioned – the thought of a cool beer – any notions the rest of them may have had to continue our aimless ramble were bombed out. We marched back up to Moto-machi 1 and into Licky's Bar. The place was pitch-black and slightly smaller than the boot of a Mini, but it was selling drink – hopefully! I called out with a hopeful 'hello' into the darkness. The call was returned but in a somewhat higher pitch. We were in business.

This guy appeared out of nowhere and began switching all the lights on. It was still very early in the afternoon but, unlike our own culture back home, the guy probably wasn't expecting any custom at this time of the day. I think he thought we were sailors. Anyway, he began connecting all these plugs up and I twigged straight away. I ordered up four bottles of *Budweiser* then said to the guy '144'. Neil Webb looked at me and said, 'What are you doing?'

'Just wait and see.' On came Simon and Garfunkel's Bridge Over Troubled Water. We were in a karaoke bar and I was on centre stage. That was it; we went right on the lash for the afternoon. We had to go back to the hotel for our evening meal with the rest of the squad and try to act sober. As we ate our food the conversation turned to what everyone was doing for tonight. 'Don't worry,' I told them, 'we've got it sorted and it's not that far away.' So the whole squad returned to Licky's. One thing we all found out very quickly was the locals love to get up and do a turn. The only problem was they were hopeless! You can't take the piss out of them though because it's seen as being very disrespectful. We just had to endure these 'singers' who sounded more like banshees with car battery clips attached to their genitalia. It was awful, but still, we had a fantastic time.

Another marvellous experience I had on that trip was the train journey we took from Kobe up to Tokyo. It was on one of their world-renowned Bullet Trains. This thing was fully air-conditioned, had upstairs and downstairs, was as smooth as marble and went like shit off a shovel. Oh yeah, and it was on time! I thought about our own rail system back home and where the hell *our* engineers and boffins had gone wrong. For a distance of some 250 miles we were only on the train for about seven minutes. I *am* exaggerating of course but this thing was awesome. We occupied the passageway downstairs because you were able to get a bevvy, which was handy.

The five star hotel we were staying in was situated right in the centre of Tokyo and was total class. The Everton boys were also using it, which was great. There were four bars within the hotel complex itself and we had been laying siege to the one which sold only bottled beer. The next day Robbo

was off doing some interviews for the local media and probably making millions of pounds for himself. The rest of us
had gone into the bottle bar again and a round of twelve Buds
was ordered up, and so it went, round by round. Later on we
were like, 'Who's gonna sign for this in Robbo's absence?'
Eventually, Steve Bruce signed for it and thought nothing more
of it. What had happened, going back to the issue we'd had
with the club regarding daily money allowances and the £500
etc, was resolved in a roundabout way when they said, 'Look,
we can't give *you* the money as such but you can put costs
onto the sponsor's bill.' The next morning we were sitting at
breakfast and Fergie comes in. 'Brucie,' he says, 'did you
drink 144 bottles of Bud yesterday?' Brucie was all flustered
and choking on his tongue. The boss carried on, 'Well you've
signed for it!'

Brucie finally got some words out and muttered back, 'Er,
yeah, well Robbo wasn't there.'

'So did I give you permission to sign for it?'

'Ah but . . .'

Fergie cut in, 'Never mind, ah but, ah but!' By this time the
rest of us were creasing ourselves, that is, once we'd realised
Fergie was winding him up.

While we were staying in Tokyo we thought it would be a
great idea to visit the Disneyland theme park but Fergie
knocked that right on the head. He didn't want anyone getting
injured unnecessarily while playing on roller-coasters and the
like so instead he came up with a plan to appease us and
decided we'd all go and see The Three Degrees in concert.
Everyone was like, 'Fuck this for a joke! The Three Degrees?
We can't tell our wives this one!' The venue was massive but
only around a third full. Brian McClair didn't fancy singing

along to 'When Will I See You Again' and buggered off up to the back stalls to sprawl across three seats for a kip. I have to admit, I quite enjoyed them myself. It got even better when we got introduced to them at the end and the photographers were all over the place snapping away. Fergie thought this was wonderful. I'm not sure the rest of the lads would have described it like that though.

I played in the match against Japan which took place at a baseball ground. That was something different. That final game had a happy outcome when we won 1-0 through a Mark Robins goal. All in all, the entire trip was a magnificent experience with some great laughs along the way and I'm glad I was given the opportunity to be a part of it. For the return journey home we were scheduled to fly via Alaska which I was very excited about. It didn't disappoint, in fact it was majestic.

As part of my transfer deal it was agreed that Fergie would take a team down to play Bristol City in a pre-season friendly and a few days after arriving back in England we travelled there for the match. I hadn't been aware of this arrangement until a week or so before but it was great to meet up with Joe and the boys again. My best mate at City, Andy Llewellyn, was playing directly opposite me at right back so before we kicked off we made a pact not to go near one another. It was probably the friendliest friendly ever.

15

PLAYING IN THE SHADOWS

When the 89/90 season kicked off I wasn't too surprised when I didn't make the first team pool for the opening match which, I might add, couldn't have been any tougher – a home tie against defending champions Arsenal. The Gunners had won the English Division One title in truly sensational circumstances when Michael Thomas scored with virtually the last kick of the ball against Liverpool to seal a 2-0 victory and snatch the trophy away from Anfield. I wasn't involved but you still had to report into Old Trafford. I went into the dressing room about quarter-to two and noticed a guy standing with a club blazer on. I'd never seen this man in my life and wondered why everything was quiet. I said to Brian McClair, 'Hey Choccy, who's that?'

'Shhhh, he's just bought the club,' he replied.

'Fuck off,' I said, 'he's not got enough money to buy *this* club!' He heard me. It was Michael Knighton. This was the business tycoon who was allegedly going to invest heavily in the club and bring the great days back. With a £20 million takeover bid tabled he'd reportedly done the deal already with Chairman Martin Edwards. This was a complete and utter surprise to all of us. However, as the days and weeks progressed, his financial backers evaporated into thin air and the whole thing fell on its arse. Something went on behind the scenes and he ended up being made a director at Man United, a post he held for a few years.

It quickly became evident that Michael Knighton was a tad eccentric, with maybe a couple of bolts missing. Most football fans will now know he went onto the pitch and proceeded to wow the fans with a keepie-up display, which he topped off by blasting the ball into an empty net down at the Stretford End. He thought he was fuckin' Pele! After a failed attempt as a professional footballer, this was the closest he was going to get to living out his dream. The early euphoria which he'd created as a direct result of his claims soon vanished and was replaced with fury and resentment. Following our little 'introduction' to each other in the dressing room that day, any time I was walking along the corridors at Old Trafford and he was walking towards me he'd look up at the roof and walk straight past. I thought, 'Fuck you pal, I've sussed you *right* out and have done right from the start!'

Incidentally, that first match, United swept Arsenal aside with a 4-1 demolition job. Webbie (Neil Webb) scored a twenty-five-yard wonder goal on his debut. As the weeks passed by I knew there was no way back into the first team although I did come on as a sub in one match but, really, I'd resigned myself to reserve football and playing in the shadows. With Paul Ince soon to be signing and young Lee Sharpe now taking on the role of left-winger, I guess I was surplus to requirements. When United faced their derby rivals Man City at Maine Road late in September, the pressure was already mounting on Fergie and the daggers were being sharpened.

The team's inconsistent start had come in for some heavy criticism and the gaffer had to stand and take what was being thrown at him. Come the end of that Man City tie even Fergie must have felt his neck was on the block and the executioner was teeing up for the fatal blow. United were destroyed 5-1 in what must have been one of their heaviest derby defeats ever.

The bad form continued right up until the end of 1989 with sections of the support and various journalists calling for his head. The stress must have been unbearable and he admitted himself it was the worst period he had ever endured during his footballing career. There was the infamous banner unfurled at a match at Old Trafford stating 'THREE YEARS OF EXCUSES AND IT'S STILL CRAP. TA RA FERGIE'. I often wonder how these fans and media folk must feel now when they look back and recall themselves running with the pack and baying for Fergie's blood. You can just hear them squirming saying, 'No, I wasn't one of those who called for him to be sacked!' He's only gone and turned out to be *the* most successful football manager on the planet!

We as players knew more than anyone else the intense pressure he was under at that particular time to produce results and yet he still never took it out on his men. I can only comment from a personal point of view, but I firmly believe he still had the backing of all the players, not least the guys whom he had signed. They demonstrated this with a do-or-die performance in the game which many people have since popularly labelled 'the match that saved his career'. It was of course the third round FA Cup tie away to Nottingham Forest on Sunday, 7 January 1990. I actually made the bench for this one but didn't play any part in the match. I think I was only pulled in as a last resort for cover because we had such a long injury list. Young Mark Robins scored the only goal of the game to put us through to the next round and give our manager the slightest of breathing spaces. I'm sure Fergie, looking back on it now, would be the first to admit the colossal significance of that result. It was nonetheless still only *one* positive result and there was a hellish long way to go yet.

In that same month I was out with the reserves for training on a Monday morning and what we used to do first thing was just roll the balls out and try and clobber someone in the nut with them. Well I launched this one and straight away a sharp pain tore through my groin area. I thought, 'Jesus Christ that was sore!' I limped my way through the rest of the session then at the end I made the decision to delay telling Fergie until the next morning. When Lee and I had first moved into the house in Prestwich I'd gone down to the local pub called The Grapes to suss it out and have a few pints. It was only 200 yards away from us and as time went on I began to get more and more acquainted with it. It was owned by the Atomic Kitten singer Jenny Frost's father who was a Scouser – in a Manchester boozer! There was a psychiatric hospital situated nearby and a load of the nurses used to go there for a drink. I'm sure they were actually patients wearing nurses' uniforms that were let out for some recreation – they were all bonkers! I showed them all how to play the game 'Spoof' which was a guessing game involving three coins. There were some unbelievable drinking sessions.

Well, after I'd done my groin in that morning I headed for the pub and had a good skinful. When I got home the phone went so I said to Lee (who was pregnant at the time), 'You'd better get that.' She picked it up then covered the mouthpiece and said very quietly to me, 'It's Fergie.' I nearly had kittens! I instantly tried putting the sober head on and switching my dialogue to 'articulate mode'. As I took the phone I was thinking, 'I hope he doesn't smell my breath down the other end.'

'All right boss?' I asked, keeping it short and sweet.

'Ralph,' he said, 'Lou Macari is struggling for players down at West Ham and he's asked me if I could loan him a winger. I thought about you and figured some first team action would be good, get you some games.'

'OK boss.'

'Get yourself down to London tomorrow.'

I was in a right pickle now. I was pished and injured and all I could think of was, 'How do I get out of this?' I couldn't. I got myself sorted out and headed off down south. The Hammers had been relegated to Division Two the previous season and Lou was having a hard time getting results. Anyway, West Ham were drawn against Derby County in the League Cup so I was put on the subs bench and thought, 'Great, I won't be used.' I'm sure the score was tied at 1-1 and with about eight minutes remaining I got the nod to go on. 'Fuck's sake that's all I need!' I didn't want the ball near me and managed to stay out of harm's way. The only touch I got was when the ball hit off me! I spent the next month there playing in the reserves but it was hopeless, I just couldn't run. I still couldn't tell anyone. In truth, this is the first time I've spoken about what really happened.

During my short period at Upton Park a huge scandal (not involving West Ham I may add) had been brewing which was about to explode onto the public stage. It involved Lou Macari and Brian Hillier, who was Chairman at Lou's former club

Swindon Town. There were all sorts of allegations flying about regarding illegal betting and Inland Revenue tax payment irregularities. After being fined £1,000 in court Macari stepped down as manager of West Ham and was replaced by Billy Bonds. Lou was later cleared of any wrongdoing. A week after that drama and the very last day of my loan period and who are the Hammers due to play – Swindon Town! I thought, 'Forget it! I'm not going away down to Swindon just to watch a match.' I travelled back up to Prestwich and hit The Grapes.

I reported back at Man United on the Monday and complained to the physio that my groin was sore. I said, 'I think I've pulled something.'

'How did that happen?' he asked.

'Ach Wee Louie,' I replied, 'all he did was run us up and down steps and do sit-ups and everything.'

'Right, we'd better get that looked at.' He sent me to Wythenshawe Hospital to have it examined. They had this great big machine which had come from Holland and was located in the back of an artic lorry so I was wheeled in for a full scan and the woman sat reading it. She said, 'You've got a tear, like a hernia.' I had to bite my lip. What I wanted to say was, 'I could have bloody told you that!' It did, however, highlight how bad the injury was. I got back and I asked our physio, 'See that new machine out there, from Holland? How much does that cost to have that done?'

He said, 'About ten grand.'

I nearly hit the deck and thought, 'Fuck me! I could have told them myself and saved them all that dough!' So there I was waiting on an operation and totally out of commission. I approached the physio just about every day asking when the operation was due. He told me I'd have to see the club doctor.

Now, two of the young lads had had the operation for the same condition and I'd observed how they'd struggled to recover. He referred me to a consultant who explained what the operation would entail. He was going to cut me in two separate places, one in the groin and one lower down my inner thigh which he said was necessary for relieving the pressure. I told him straight to his face, 'No way, you're not cutting me there (on the thigh). If you cut me whilst under anaesthetic I'll have you sued.' He was not happy at all with my reaction. When I eventually went in for the operation sometime during April he came through and said, 'We've had a think about things and we're not going to cut you down there.'

I said, 'I've told you that already!' After the op I woke up the following day and the surgeon told me everything had gone fine and if I needed to rest it was no problem and he'd come back tomorrow to get me up and mobile. I felt really well so I ended up going for a wander outside the hospital. He returned the next day and asked, 'How are you feeling? Do you fancy having a little walk up and down the stairs?' I told him I'd already done that and witnessed the resultant look of surprise on his face.

'Oh, OK then. In that case Mr Milne you can go home if you want.'

'Yes I'd like that. My girlfriend is pregnant.'

That was on the Thursday so when I reported in at the Cliff training ground on the Monday Archie (Knox) confronted me and said, 'You're some boy you. I came up to see you and you'd buggered off!' He'd come up in the afternoon to visit but I was already gone. We both had a laugh about it. That was my season effectively over though. Things really went downhill from there and I hit the drink hard.

165

At this point in my life, my enthusiasm for the game of football had drained considerably. I was asking myself questions about my whole attitude and professionalism towards the game and I didn't have any answers. The old hunger, sparkle and desire had long gone, my inspiration had melted away like the snows of spring and the fire in my belly was extinguished. It was probably debatable whether I noticed these things happening or whether I even cared. However, I will state quite frankly, I wasn't unhappy and I hadn't retreated in on myself. The circumstances were what they were and I just went with the flow.

I was very surprised therefore when Fergie pulled me in and offered me another year's contract. With my present one due to run out on 1 July, I was kind of waiting in limbo to see what the club would say. If I'm honest I really did not expect it to be renewed. Perhaps they'd offered it because I'd been injured and missed five months of the season, who knows, but I was definitely happy to stay. I loved life in Manchester.

Whenever Robbo used to call a 'team meeting' that was the cue to go out for a bevvy. On one such occasion we found ourselves in a situation that can only be described as completely bizarre but also had the potential to be somewhat damaging for all those involved. It was midweek and we didn't have a game (not that I was able anyway!) so a squad of us went down to a hotel in Sale, on the south side of Manchester, which was run by one of Robbo's mates. After a couple of beers there we went along the road to another pub and couldn't believe our eyes when we walked in. A whole squad of Man City boys were in drinking and the utter surprise shown on their faces was just as pronounced as our own.

We all ended up having a few beers and a laugh together.

Looking around the joint, this unique scene was hard to take in and felt totally surreal. I think everyone was well aware of the implications this chance meeting could have. It was a paparazzi's dream and if the press had turned up we would all have been well and truly in the shit! God only knows how both clubs would have dealt with that. It would certainly have given the fans something to talk about. Fair play to the barman though for he could quite easily have picked up his phone and earned himself a very healthy little earner for an 'exclusive'. I'm sure if anyone *had* been snooping about with a camera the doors would have been bolted and the guilty snapper would have received some 'correctional advice' on mending the errors of his ways!

The first team's erratic form in the League continued and I suppose the only saving grace for Fergie was the progress made in the FA Cup. Rumours continued to fly around whether he would be sacked and I think it is fair comment to suggest that exit from the Cup competition would have resulted in his departure, even though the board were allegedly still backing him. How many times have we heard that statement in football and the very next day a manager is sacked?

Having reached the semis against what would be termed 'weaker' opposition, the excitement began to grow at the prospect of reaching the final. Nothing was being taken for granted, however, which was maybe just as well for it took a replay to overcome Oldham Athletic. In the first game Man U were very lucky to escape with a 3-3 draw. The team were now in the final and due to face Londoners Crystal Palace on the day before my twenty-ninth birthday. I approached Alex Ferguson and said, 'Boss, I know I'm not involved but is there any chance I can go to the Cup Final with the boys?'

'Ralph,' he said, 'you were subbie against Forest, you're entitled to three guests.' I thought, 'That's brilliant!' The first team flew down to London on the Thursday or the Friday. On the Saturday morning I flew down with Lee Sharpe and Colin Gibson and my guests who were Lee and our next-door neighbours. The club had spared no expense and took staff and everyone connected. It must have cost them a small fortune and many of us stayed in the same hotel whilst the team stayed in the plush Royal Lancaster Hotel.

We were coached to a sun-baked Wembley Stadium and watched all the drama unfold in a pulsating encounter which had to go into extra time after finishing all square at 2-2. When Ian Wright scored his second and made it 3-2 it began to look desperate for us as the game went into its final period. There was no need to worry though as Sparky scored his second, coolly slotting home the equaliser which took the game to a replay. It had been end-to-end stuff and was packed full of incident swinging first one way then the other, but for Big Jazzer (Jim Leighton) in the goal it had been a bit of a night-mare and one game he'd rather forget. He'd come in for criticism over some displays during the season and this game sadly proved to be his last for United.

Following the game we went to a gala ball which went on all night then next morning we all boarded a very fancy train for the journey home. I said to a steward when I got on, 'I want you to look after me today, it's my birthday.' The next thing the champagne was flowing and we were all steaming. Back in Manchester we arrived at Old Trafford where an open-top bus was waiting to take the squad around the city. The only problem was there was no cup to parade! It was a strange situation but everyone made the most of it. I remember going downstairs on the bus and speaking to Sir Matt Busby for ten minutes or so. When I went back upstairs I sat at the back with the lads but unfortunately the drink had run out. I spotted Michael Knighton who was sitting at the front clutching a bottle of champagne. I turned to Robbo and said, 'Watch this. Hey Mikey, don't sit up there on your own, come down here and sit with the lads and bring that fuckin' bottle!' He joined the company and we helped demolish his champagne. After that I was his best mate. I was the only one he'd speak to.

The replay was held the following Thursday but this time I was only allowed one guest so my mate Keith, who was Man United daft, came along. Prior to travelling I'd been at Old Trafford when a staff member approached me and said, 'I believe you have a job to do Ralph?'

'Well, nobody's told me,' I replied, a little confused.

'The manager says you've got to look after all these tickets.'

I thought for a second then said, 'Oh yes, I forgot all about that, no problem.' I can't remember how many I was given, possibly forty. These were the tickets for the players' wives etc. to access all areas and get up to the suite at the end of the game. The thought occurred to me that 'Surely, no one would stop the players' wives going anywhere in Wembley Stadium?' The wee wheelies began turning in my head then I said, 'Fuck it. I'm going to hand them all out!' I started making phone calls to friends in Bristol and elsewhere. Down at the ground people were turning up from all over for their 'complimentaries'. It was mental!

I said to Keith, 'Right, see that door there at the tunnel? Wait five minutes, show the guy your pass then there's another doorway further up on the right, just wait for me there.'

I left him and went away into the dressing room to wish the lads well. They were very upbeat and in confident mood. Fergie said to me, 'Ralph, did you sort all those tickets out?'

'Yeah, it's all done boss.' I then said to him, 'Hey boss, do you realise, I've been in five cup finals and never won one yet?'

'Get out this fuckin' dressing room!' he shouted. I made a quick exit and was walking up the tunnel when I noticed Keith standing in the doorway. He was gesturing to me but I could feel Fergie's eyes burning a hole in my back. As I approached him I said quietly, 'Is Fergie looking at me?' He nodded back.

'You've got me in a right pile of shite. You'd be as well going out onto the pitch and savouring the whole moment now!'

The next thing, he *did* go out onto the pitch and was up at the Man U end giving it large. People were asking themselves, 'Is this a new director or something?' Talk about seizing the moment, I could have strangled him! I took full advantage of the 'access all areas' myself and made for the main function suite above the tunnel, which was just amazing. This was my idea of how football *should* be watched and we enjoyed the fantastic hospitality to the utmost. And the champagne tasted all the sweeter when Lee Martin burst into the box in the second half and thrashed a shot high into the roof of the net for the winner and only goal of the game.

I was really chuffed for the lads but especially Fergie. He had been through hell the past season and had shouldered the responsibility like a true leader. I'm sure there were times when he must have doubted his own ability but he stuck with the task and secured his first silverware for the club. The history books have shown just what a momentous win it was for Manchester United. Having finished in a very poor position of thirteenth in the League, defeat in the Cup was unthinkable.

Thankfully, all the wives and girlfriends had managed to get into the match and there were no reports filtering back about confrontations between them and security staff. I mean, you could just imagine Robbo's wife being refused entry into somewhere – it just wasn't going to happen. I'd got away with it and I was feeling quite pleased with myself. Everyone connected with the club travelled back on the train which turned into one big rolling party. I was sitting beside Keith when I clocked the manager who was making his way up the train with the Cup full of champagne. He stopped beside me and said, 'Here Ralph.' I took the Cup from him and sipped on the champagne then said, 'Congratulations boss.' I nearly fell off my seat when he turned to my mate and said, 'Here you are Keith.'

'Aw congratulations Mr Ferguson, great game blah, blah, blah.'

Fergie waited till he finished then said, 'Did you enjoy yourself out on the pitch today?'

I sat there half-cringing, half-laughing and thought, 'It's just as well we won that Cup or I'd have been sacked!' It was absolutely brilliant and showed the great humour he possessed. There were certainly no flies on him. The fact he'd gone to the bother of finding out his name then with killer timing had delivered the *coup de grace*, it was brilliant!

16

HAVE BOOTS WILL TRAVEL

The pre-season training began for the 90/91 campaign but I wasn't at the races. Trying to rebuild six months worth of idleness and hard living in the space of three weeks just wasn't going to happen. Archie Knox asked me how I was feeling but I was still struggling to even run at half pace. By now my chances of regaining the high standard of fitness needed for playing for Man United (even if it was the reserves) were grim indeed. As any player will tell you, the older you get the harder it is to get that fitness back once it goes. I'm not saying it can't be done though. It just needs a lot more motivation and focus to achieve it. I was lacking in both. The injury had knocked the stuffing out of me and I was filling my downtime with alcohol. Off-field there was a much more serious event happening and Lee gave birth to our son Robert George Milne (named after both our fathers) on 27 August, a beautiful wee bundle.

As the weeks and months rolled on there was only me and Jim (Leighton) from the first team in the dressing room. Fergie had dropped him after the 3-3 draw in the FA Cup final and replaced him with Les Sealey for the replay. I don't think Jim ever regained his first team place but at least he was playing for the reserves. I wasn't even turning out for them. Fergie and Archie didn't bother with me because they knew I was on the piss and probably a lost cause.

I often think back and wished they *had* given me a good kick up the arse and told me to get a grip but they obviously felt it was too late and they were possibly correct. My mindset was miles away from playing football. The reserve team manager was understandably losing patience and after training in the morning he used to say to me, 'Right, back for training in the afternoon.'

I'd tell him, 'I'm not coming back for training this afternoon.'

'I'll go and tell the manager (Fergie),' he'd threaten.

'Go and tell the manager, in fact I'll tell him myself.' Thankfully, it never did get to that. He didn't like me though and I felt the same way about him.

Sometime in the February of 1991 he came and asked me if I would go and play in the reserves against Sheffield United at Bramall Lane. It was the last time I would turn out for the club and I scored a cracker. Fergie's son Darren was playing that day and I told him to flick the ball to me as we were attacking. I hit a ferocious volley with my left which screamed right into the top corner. It was like a final statement – out with a bang.

As for the first team, Fergie was slowly beginning to make progress and win over those who were still critical of him. In the April of 91 the club reached the final of the League Cup but were surprisingly beaten by Sheffield Wednesday who were in Division Two. The defeat was all the harder to take as Wednesday were managed by ex-United manager Ron

Atkinson. A few days later, however, the disappointment of that loss was soothed a great deal when they secured a place in the final of the European Cup Winners' Cup after beating Legia Warsaw over two legs.

The club was buzzing at the prospect of facing Barcelona in Rotterdam and a final League placing of sixth was a step in the right direction. I knew I'd be out the Old Trafford door when my contract was up in June and Fergie pulled me into his office to confirm it but I was allowed to travel to Holland in May and cheer on the lads. Sparky did the damage scoring both goals in a 2-1 win to send the travelling army of fans into ecstasy. The Alex Ferguson era had now begun in earnest!

For me, the last year had been a lost one and my downward spiral had gathered momentum. Even though I knew it was over I didn't want to hear those words when Fergie told me. It was absurd but I just wanted things to continue as they were but, of course, that was impossible. I had been collecting a wage for doing virtually nothing and it was amazing that I was allowed to carry on in that manner. No employer on this planet can operate like that and I had to go. There was in fact a large-scale clear-out that summer and many players experienced the same fate as I did.

I had to hand back the club car and I made sure I left only a drop of fuel in the engine. I dropped it off to be picked up by the groundsman whom I was very friendly with. I pissed myself laughing when I next met up with him. He said, 'Ralph you c***. I got ten feet along the road in your car and the bloody thing conked out. Thanks to you I had to go and find a jerrycan to get fuel to get it moving again!'

When I look back on my time at Man U I don't think I did a bad job, when I was playing that is. I was given an opportunity to play for the most famous club in the world, albeit at a time when they were in obvious disarray. Playing left wing wasn't my favoured position but I would have played anywhere to get a game. I came in for some heavy criticism from a section of the support and have been labelled in some quarters as 'one of the worst signings ever for Man United'. To those knockers I will say this – my contributions during those games in which I played were no less than those of my fellow team mates.

The simple fact is the team did not function as a unit and did not gel together. That was not the fault of any one individual, it just wasn't the correct blend and Fergie knew that. At a mere £170,000, my signing fee was never going to burst the bank of Manchester United. However, I was playing alongside guys, some of whom were seasoned internationalists and worth a hell of a lot more than I was but still weren't able to produce match-winning performances consistently. There's no denying all of these guys could play, myself included, but it just wasn't happening as a team.

A core of United fans started singing 'Ralphie, Ralphie, Ralphie' during my early games and continued to do so throughout but, when we weren't doing so well, certain sections singled me out for the booing treatment. I don't know, perhaps they needed a scapegoat for a whole team who weren't playing particularly well. The other side to my Man United career is a whole different story, as you will have gathered, and for that I only have myself to blame.

For Alex 'Fergie' Ferguson I have only the utmost respect. I thank him for giving me a chapter in my life which I will always look back on fondly – and that includes the football! I'm glad I was there at a period when he was laying the foundations towards becoming one of the most successful football managers ever. I would have loved to have worked under him when I was in my prime and at my most deadly.

Life away from United meant I had no steady income to provide for my family. I was drinking every day and hitting the bookies, which wasn't the kind of behaviour that was going to help our situation. At that moment I felt my life had no direction. I chose to ignore the damage I was doing and carry on regardless. At thirty years old, the thought of going back out into the 'big bad world' scared me a little. There was a serious need for me to find work and the only work I'd ever known was professional football. The problem I had was that I was in no fit state to do so. The club had given me a period in which to sort myself out and try and secure another club. I had a very brief spell at Third Division Bury, but that didn't work out.

Then the inevitable happened and our house was repossessed. Lee, Robert and I moved back down to the Bristol area, but any hopes of things changing for the better soon dissolved and I began hitting the boozer on a daily basis. I was featured in a newspaper article which caused some controversy and indirectly led to a few offers of employment. Totally out of the blue I received a phone call from a guy representing the Turkish team Ankaragucu asking if I'd be interested in going over for a trial. I don't know if it was just a coincidence with the piece in the newspaper but he'd obviously gone into the database to check out players who were available on free transfers. I thought about it quickly then told him, 'Yes.'

I needed to get out of the rut I was in and decided a change of scenery would do me good. At the back of my mind I knew there was no way they'd sign me but I thought 'What the hell, I'll go and have a wee holiday anyway.' An hour later the phone went again and this time it was a guy from Shelbourne FC in Ireland asking the same question. I couldn't believe it, nothing for ages then two offers back-to-back. I'd already given the Turkish guy my word so Ankara it was.

I flew over to Istanbul and was met by a couple of club officials. We exchanged pleasantries then they took me down to the Bosphorus area and a restaurant right by the water. The food was out of this world. I think it cost something like seventeen quid. The equivalent over here would have been about a hundred and fifty quid! After we'd eaten, one of the guys asked me, 'You drink raki?'

'No, no I don't drink.' If I'd had a Pinocchio nose I would have knocked them both off their seats! I had to try and make a good impression.

'OK, tonight, we take you to a five-star hotel then tomorrow we fly to Ankara.'

Five-star hotel my arse! This was the Turkish version of *Fawlty Towers*. I was grateful though that they had splashed out and put me up in a five-star – I'd hate to have seen the three-star!

As a city Istanbul was intense. I'd been to places like Rome, Bangkok and Tokyo, but this took the biscuit. I just don't know how people can live in such a manic and over-crowded environment. We flew out the next day to the capital city and after arriving I quickly became aware of the chaotic traffic on the roads. I think their local law states you must beep your horn every three seconds. It was a nightmare. The facilities at the club were top notch and they had a compound where the young players were housed so they gave me a room there. I couldn't fault the people there, they were extremely friendly.

One of the young guys even brought a TV into my room. Unfortunately it was all in Turkish, but it was a nice gesture.

Ankaragucu were sitting about mid-table in the top division at the time. The Turkish national side were playing England in some Euro qualifier so the team were on a two week break from League business. At the training ground I was amazed to see large crowds turn out to watch us being put through our paces. I was breathing out of my arse and knew it wasn't going to happen. One of the club officials had spotted me with tins of Coke which I'd bought myself and he explained that I don't pay for a thing while I was there. He then handed me a load of Turkish lira. I knew you could be a millionaire out there with their currency but this was in fact a fair whack of money I'd been given.

On the Saturday morning we played a practice match and I had a decent game. The wheelies started going in my head and I thought, 'Maybe they *will* offer me a contract.' I didn't know about the place though. It reminded me of the film *Midnight Express* and I suppose it was a bit of a culture shock, what with all the eerie prayer chanting I'd heard the previous evening echoing around. The following Monday a guy took me into the office and basically told me 'no chance'. He said, 'When do you want to go home?'

'Tomorrow,' I said.

'No, no flights. Not any till Wednesday.'

I left him and jumped straight into a taxi. I said to the driver, 'You take me to European bar?' I got dropped off and went into this bar which was pitch-black. It was like déjà-vu with that bar in Japan. I shouted out and eventually a guy appears. 'Can I have a Budweiser please?' He put all the lights on and I asked him if this was a European bar.

'No, this no European bar. I get my son.'

I thought, 'What the fuck are we getting here?'

His son came out and said, 'You go Bar Telescope.'

I jumped in a taxi and headed for this mysterious Bar Telescope. I was in the car for nearly three-quarters of an hour and the journey only cost something like a pound. There was a massive bouncer standing on the door, immaculately dressed with dickey bow the lot and here's me wandering in with jeans on. Everyone inside was wearing suits and I thought, 'Fuck me, what is this?'

The whole bar was decorated with ornamental fish tanks containing hundreds of tropical fish. I ordered up a beer and took in the surroundings. After a while I became aware of the bouncer who kept sticking his head in the door and watching me. I was beginning to worry he was looking for some punch-bag practice. The rest of the clientele were European and were a mixture of businessmen and pilots. I ordered another drink at the bar and the barman said, 'You have sixteen drinks?'

'Yeah, don't worry Jim.' It was all on a tab and I'm sure he was worried I was gonna do a runner; hence the reason for Bluto the Doorman's agitated state. I clocked the cocktail list hanging on the wall behind him and said, 'Right, I'm going to start there (at the top) and finish there (at the bottom).' He just stared back at me with a funny look. I was well on at the end of the session and went to square him up. It came to something like twenty-five quid so I took the money from the wedge I had and gave him a good tip. He got me a taxi and made sure I was sorted for the journey back. At the training ground the next morning they asked me if I was taking part. I told them I didn't want to risk getting injured and they reluctantly accepted that. When the squad had finished their stint

179

I went and got one of the young lads to take me back up to Bar Telescope. I walked in and the same guy who'd served me the previous night greeted me warmly and couldn't do enough for me. I ended up blootered!

I remember tapping on the fish tanks saying, 'Here fishy fishy.' I don't remember if they answered back or not. That wasn't the end of it though and I found myself in a night-club later, although my dancing performance remains a hazy memory. I do recall the place was somewhat dodgy and I managed to extract myself before things got *really* messy. Ankara was a great experience but I'm not sure I could have hacked life out there for a year or even six months.

On my return to England I had another call shortly afterwards, this time from Denmark. A team called Esbjerg wanted me to go over for a trial and I gladly obliged. Again, I knew there was no way they'd want me but I wasn't passing up the chance of another jolly, especially to Scandinavia! I boarded the ship and settled in for the twenty-four-hour ferry crossing to Esbjerg, which was marvellous. The club put me through my paces in a couple of arranged games in Copenhagen but it was a case of 'no thanks Mr Milne'. I made my way back to the hotel and ordered up the most expensive bottle of champagne and meal on the menu then went into the city and got pissed. The next day was spent nursing a hangover travelling back to England and back to reality once more.

17

HONG KONG THEN BUST

There then followed a period of nothing, no offers, and I honestly thought that was it, it was time to hang up the boots. You can imagine my astonishment then when one day I picked up the phone and listened as some guy asked me in very broken English if I wanted to play football in Hong Kong for Sing Tao football team? I thought someone was at the capers and winding me up. Anyway, I said yes then asked who it was.

'My name is Mr Wu. You speak to my daughter.'

His daughter came on and spoke very good English. She asked if I could come for a trial in Ashford in Kent. Her dad owned a restaurant there and it was an area which I knew well from living in Crayford when I was with Charlton. I told her that I wasn't prepared to travel all the way to Kent for a trial so she said she'd discuss the matter with her father and they would phone back. A little later Mr Wu spoke again and arranged to meet me at some Tie Rack stall near a railway station. I didn't know where the hell he was on about but after some confusion we eventually sorted it out and agreed to meet at Victoria Station. I chucked my boots and gear in a bag and off I went to see what the script was. I asked my mate Gerry to come along and act as my agent.

It turned out the guy was an ex-player with the team and now acted as a kind of middle man. The need for a trial became apparent as he explained a year earlier an English guy who was carrying an injury, signed a contract and went out. He broke down in training on the first day and they had to keep him for the year. He never kicked a ball the whole time he was out there. They'd obviously learned their lesson and wanted to make sure you could play and were fit. There was supposed to be another guy having a trial with me but he never showed up. Mr Wu's daughter was only about fifteen or sixteen and had travelled up with him to translate. He was all ready for action and must have made the journey in his kit. We went into St James's Park and he pointed out a pavilion which was about half a mile away where I could get changed.

'I'm not going away over there to change!' I exclaimed, so I went and stood under a nearby tree and got stripped. I think he thought I was nuts. He took a ball out of his holdall and said, 'We kick ball.'

'What do you mean, we kick ball?' We started passing it back and forth to each other then he said, 'You do high kicking, long kicking.' I looked at him and thought, 'What the hell is he on about now?' It was all very confusing. He wanted me to play some long passes and he backed off for a distance. I fired this thing; it was going like a rocket and he began back-pedalling in order to try and chest it down. It hit him clean in the face and decked him! I couldn't stop laughing. Gerry was telling me to stop but I couldn't help it, it was hilarious. Next thing he says, 'OK, me and you, one against one.'

I took the ball up to him and nutmegged him. Gerry piped

up again and told me not to take the piss out of him. When my little 'trial' was over he said, 'Now we talk,' so we dropped into a nearby cafe and he explained the situation. He took out a sheet of A4-sized paper which had all the contract details numbered one to ten. At the top of the list was all the basic stuff like payment for flights, accommodation etc. Number four was titled 'salary' and was left blank. He discussed all the other conditions and explained the contract was for a year then he returned to number four.

'OK, how much money do you want?'

'I don't know what you're paying so how can I tell you?' I replied. There was a moment's pause then I asked, 'What's your top salary?'

'Four to 450 (British pounds).'

'I'll take the 450,' I said.

'Oh no, no, no. Jason and Paul are only on 350!'

'I don't know who the hell Jason and Paul are but, as I'm a senior player, I'll be wanting your top salary.'

Gerry was kicking me under the table but I just thought 'Bollocks, I'm having the 450.' It all went uncomfortably silent for about ten minutes after that, but I wasn't too bothered, I had nothing to lose. In the end Mr Wu spoke and said, 'OK, I give you 450.'

That's just what I wanted to hear and we shook hands. Some time after our meeting I received another phone call from him asking me to pick up my flight ticket in London. There was no way I was going to do that and I told him so. Couldn't he just leave it at a desk in the airport and I'd collect it there? He was scared it would be stolen so that sensible idea was knocked on the head. The conversation was going nowhere so I asked if anyone else was going out there. He gave me a number for a guy up in Coventry called Simon who was also travelling.

I phoned him up and introduced myself then asked if he was picking up his ticket and if so, could he get mine and I'd meet him in the terminal on the day we were due to fly out. It worked out perfectly as he was going to stay at his brother's house in London then collect the tickets. He was only nineteen and had been given a 'free' from Coventry City. He told me he played as a centre forward and was about 6ft 2in.

On the day of our departure I went up to Heathrow and was strolling up and down the terminal searching for a guy who looked like a footballer. It was unclear exactly where we'd meet but I clocked this guy wearing a tracksuit so I wandered over and asked, 'Are you Simon?' It was indeed. All his family members had turned up to see him off and I stood there thinking, 'Is this guy for real?'

Now, I hadn't been keeping myself in any great shape over the last few years but I looked at this young man with his stooped shoulders and pot-belly and came to the conclusion there may be hope for me yet. He said his goodbyes to his family then we made our way through to the departure lounge and to the bar. 'Right,' I said, 'we'll need to watch what we're doing so we'll just have a couple. The press are sure to be waiting at Kai Tak Airport for interviews and I don't want to be reeking of ale.' As we sat there he said, 'I can't wait to get out there.'

'Yeah, it should be good,' I answered. 'We'll see what happens.' He then took the conversation off on a completely different tangent and said he was going to buy some sort of games console, possibly a Super Nintendo or something. I didn't have a clue what he was talking about. He assured me they were half price in Hong Kong which was great – I'd maybe get two myself! I let his statement go but three hours later when we were cruising at around 40,000 feet I wished I'd had a parachute on so I could get off the plane! Young Simon was seriously doing my head in talking constant shite and we still had a good nine or ten hours to go! During the course of our riveting exchanges of topical drivel he told me that the guy who had binned him from Coventry was none other than Brian Eastwick, the same coach I'd worked under at Charlton who had passed on such expert training methods as 'stand it up in the corner' etc.

Things did liven up a little on the flight but this wasn't down to my new 'friend' falling asleep and me following it up with cartwheels down the middle aisle. No, the 'fasten seat belts' signs flashed above our heads as a warning was announced from the captain that we were about to enter into a tropical storm and things may get 'slightly bumpy'. His microphone must have got cut off due to the deteriorating weather conditions because after 'slightly bumpy' he should have added 'to begin with, then turning positively horrendous' for the plane was soon being strongly buffeted then dropping and rising like the biggest roller-coaster ride ever. I thought Simon was delivering a baby next to me; he was in a hell of a state.

'What's the matter with you?' I asked.

'I don't like this, I don't like this!'

He then informed me that he'd never been on a plane before. The fact we were about to land on one of the most infamous and hair-raising runways in the world didn't help matters very much either! To be honest, I don't think he'd been outside of Coventry all that often and was a bit wet behind the ears.

The landing was bordering on mental as we came in in the opposite direction from the normal approach via the mountains and descended low under the level of the towering buildings. You could just about see folk scratching their arses in their offices.

I was pretty glad myself when we finally touched down. A group from the local press was there to meet us and with them were Jason and Paul, the guys whom Mr Wu had mentioned. Paul was actually Paul Murray, who was one of the young players when I had been at Charlton. We did the press thing then I said to Paul, 'For crying out loud, get me to the nearest boozer. He's doing my bloody head in!' We sat chatting over a beer and Paul told me Jason and him were going away to Thailand. I thought he meant for pre-season training but it was for a holiday. I asked him when the pre-season did start and he said, 'Oh, about ten days' time.'

'Well what the hell am I doing here so early?'

'They like you to acclimatise and settle in,' he said.

'So you're telling me I'm stuck in that flat for ten days with *him*? No danger!'

The next day Jason and Paul took off on their holiday leaving me and Simon to suss out the area and catch up on some stamp-collecting chat. We walked for ages and ended up in the Wan Chai district, which was also home to the red light area and some of the seedier bars of Hong Kong Island. By now it was around ten o'clock at night and the place was buzzing. It is one of the proverbial 'cities that never sleep'. We were standing outside Bar San Francisco on Hennessy Road when he turned to me and said, 'I'd like to go into one of those girlie bars.' I tried to put him off and tell him they were just rip-off shops but he was still keen to have a look. I asked him how much money he had and he told me '$1,000 (Hong Kong).' I had roughly the same myself. I said to him, 'OK, we'll go in but I'll do the talking and you keep your mouth shut.'

We walked in and ordered up a couple of beers then out came the girls who indulged in a spot of pole-dancing. I clocked an absolute stunner straight away who, after a short bit of limbering up, gave me a wink. She came over and said, 'You buy me a drink?'

'Yes, I'll buy you a drink.' What they did though, was put a little drop of whisky in the bottom of a glass then they filled it up with lemonade and charged you the earth for it, paid for with these tokens you had to buy. They had a jar and they put the token in it then they hoped you'd get pissed and they'd start chucking the tokens in and, before you know it, you owed them a fortune. A refusal to square up your debt would almost certainly have you answering to the local Triads. She then asked if my friend would buy her friend a drink. His face went bright red but I assured her he would. When the other girl came over I said, 'Simon, are you buying her a drink or what?'

'You told me not to open my mouth or spend my money.'

'Get her a drink you tight c***!'

After another couple of drinks we left and once outside I asked him how much money he had left. 'Nothing,' he replied. I shook my head and just stared at him in disbelief. Yes, I'd told him to buy her a drink but it was obvious he was going to need some serious tuition on the ways of the world. I was to have a very hairy moment in that same bar some months later and it wasn't connected with any part of the female genitalia that's for sure! I will explain shortly.

With the eight hour time difference between Hong Kong and the UK Simon was finding it hard to adjust and couldn't sleep at night. He'd bought himself the games console he was after and by day he was chasing high scores while I went out gallivanting. The time eventually arrived for pre-season training to begin and we went to meet the rest of the lads. Each team was allowed five ex-pats so there was Jason and Paul, us two and a guy called Peter Guthrie who'd been a goalie at Tottenham Hotspur. We did a couple of weeks' fitness work then were due to sail over to the Chinese mainland for some warm-up games. I said to Peter Guthrie, 'Who do you normally room with?'

'The other goalie. Why?'

'Would you mind if I roomed with you? That Simon is a total balloon and I can't take any more!'

We got up there and I was very grateful when he let me share with him. The first thing I became aware of (apart from the stifling heat) was just how desperate and backward a place China was. We were just over the border in the province of Guandong but the differences between there and Hong Kong were startling. The province has since enjoyed a massive rise in economic growth and is one of the most prosperous areas in the whole of China now. In 1992, however, it was hellish!

After the first day of training they decided on one of the Chinese players to captain the club and they made me vice-captain to look after the gweilos (which translates into 'foreign devils'). This put Peter Guthrie's nose right out of joint. We trained at seven in the morning and again at five in the after-noon. The Chinese guys went and did their bit alone so we went and set up our own little exercises and routines, basic stuff like crossing to a team mate to either header or take on the chest then volley, that kind of thing. When big Simon's turn came it turned into an absolute hoot. He was jumping to head the ball and landing before it had even arrived near his head! He really wasn't joking when he said he was looking forward to getting his Super Nintendo or whatever it was. The football was definitely secondary. I thought, 'This guy has never been a player, never!'

The Chinese guys (who were down at the bottom of the field) ended up coming up to see what we were laughing at. They started laughing as well and when *they* start laughing at you, you know you're fucked. Our contracts were for a year but there was a clause which said they could bin you after three months if you weren't up to scratch. Simon wasn't going to last three minutes!

Later, when he did eventually get the heave, I asked him what he was planning to do when he got home. 'I'm going to join the police,' he replied. 'The police? You couldn't catch a cold never mind a criminal!' I don't know if he ever did get his dream job with the boys in blue.

A few days later Peter began complaining of toothache so he was taken to this shack which doubled up as a dental surgery. Nothing was sterilised and when the guy went to give Peter a needle he went bonkers. He'd been up there before (Guandong) and didn't fancy another twelve or thirteen days of it so he pulled a fast one and sailed back the next day to spend the time in a slightly more comfortable environment with his wife. I took my hat off to him, it was a classic stroke.

The hotel where we stayed was a kind of circular construction which was linked by bridges. These bridges went over a river and we used to watch these local fishermen wading out almost neck deep into the water with their nets. We were all warned not to eat the fish and if we needed any answers as to why not, the evidence presented itself to us midway through our stay. The fishermen were gone and the surface of the water was littered with dead fish! I don't suppose the local authorities were too bothered about what industrial waste went into the rivers. It was scary stuff. It certainly put me off donning the Speedos and doing a few lengths that's for sure!

While we were there we were given ten Yuan a day to go into the American restaurant in the hotel. Everything on the menu was ten Yuan, and no matter what you ordered, all you got was mince. Simon never failed to amaze me and I often wondered what was going on in that head of his. One day we were out eating at a restaurant and through the back you could see all these monkeys in cages just waiting their turn to have their heads lopped off and their brains scooped out for the 'soup of the day'. He saw them and said, 'Let's all chip in and buy one.'

'And what the fuck are you going to do with it like?'

'We'll set it free.'

I told him they were bred in captivity and as soon as you set it free it would wander off across the road only to end up in someone else's pot having enjoyed all of four minutes' freedom! He nearly got himself into right bother on another day when we were casually walking down a street. Being Europeans you kind of stood out a little but Simon was 6ft 2in with bright blond hair and stood out like a sore thumb. Local youths and children would follow us around. Some of the kids were naked which was disturbing to see and it brought home the level of poverty which was all too prevalent in this, the most densely over-populated country in the world.

He asked me if I had any money. He wanted ten Yuan to hand out to these locals. I warned him of the dangers of that and how it could put us all in jeopardy in these Chinese back-streets and told him to switch off from them. A short while later I noticed he wasn't behind me. Here he was up the street, lying on the ground being roughed up by a pack of young-sters who were rifling his pockets. One of the other lads had given him money, not knowing he was going to hand it over to the Chinese. Ten Yuan wasn't much to us but it was a fortune to them and when he took it out they just mobbed him. We had to go back up and throw them off. I called him for every-thing and made sure he realised how stupid he'd been.

On the last full day in China we were due to play Guandong Province. Back then football was just beginning to gain some real popularity and, as you can imagine, with millions of folk to choose from you're going to get some decent players. The stadiums were in stark contrast to much of their surround-ings – they were immaculate. It seemed crazy that just on the other side of the terrace walls people were struggling to survive but I suppose it's the same the world over. We kicked off and six minutes in I put us 1-0 up. About two or three minutes later I went in for a tackle and the guy caught me just above the knee with his studs and put a hole in my leg. Paul Murray came running over and said, 'Ralph, what does it feel like?'

'It feels like I've got a fuckin' hole in my leg!' They got an ambulance round and took me straight to the hospital, which was filthy. I had no option but to get it stitched. There was a guy lying next to me with his hands across his chest moaning, whom I thought had been stabbed. After a brief discussion between a club representative and a doctor the poor guy was shoved to the side and I was given priority. They attempted to pin me down but I was having none of that. I wanted to see exactly what they were doing to my leg.

I received three injections into the wound and nearly hit the roof. The pain was incredible. They were using what looked like the old glass milk bottles we used to have back home to pour water from while they cleaned the dirt out. My mind was racing thinking, 'Am I gonna get AIDS here?' They eventually had to pin me down to put the stitches in. I noticed another poor guy who had a terrible cut in his Achilles like it had been hit with a machete and I said to the nurse in a broad Dundee accent, 'Eh widda jist waited on yiz stitchin him up furst, nae baather.' She must've thought I was from another part of China the way she looked at me!

I got back to the stadium just as the game was ending. It finished in a 6-1 defeat for us so I asked Paul Murray what had happened. 'You went off,' he said, laughing. It was traditional over there to go for a meal with the opposing team after the match. You could just imagine them doing that back here after an explosive derby match! I asked some of our Chinese players what guy had lynched me during the game but they wouldn't tell me and it was maybe just as well. If I'd got into bother up there with the police I'd probably never have been seen again. It definitely had that kind of feel to it.

Next day on the boat back to Hong Kong Island, our chairman, whose name was Taigo, spoke to me then put $2,000 in my hand. His English wasn't so much 'pigeon', it fell more into the 'seagull' bracket and was very difficult to pick up but the gist of his words were 'go to a proper doctor when we get back and get your injury sorted properly.' Now I *really was* shitting myself and worrying about all sorts of diseases I may have picked up in that hospital. I found out later the hospital bill for my treatment in Guandong came to $10 which was less than a pound!

I went to see a 'proper' doctor and asked him to have a look at my wound. He examined it then asked me what I wanted. I told him I'd like him to sort it properly then re-stitch it and that I was also worried about infection from the water they'd used and was there a chance of AIDS? The guy looked at me as if I was nuts and assured me he couldn't do any better a job than I already had and the pain of re-stitching it would be horrendous. As for the water, if I'd had all my jags (which I did) then there was no problem. 'AIDS? No, Mr Milne. Come back in three weeks and I'll take the stitches out for you.' This only cost $200 so I had $1800 left. I was out of action, there were no receipts and nobody asked for the money back, so I headed straight for the boozer and drunk the lot. As I sunk the cold beers I contented myself in the knowledge that the money would not be missed as the club was owned by a huge printing company.

It was a great little set up out there as there were only ten teams in the League and they were all from Hong Kong. With each side having five ex-pats we all got to know each other and would meet up regularly to socialise. We used to train at Happy Valley racecourse where they had about five pitches and a running track. The sessions were held later in the after-noon to let the local lads finish their work. The training was a bit of a joke though.

I remember one hilarious episode when the training was moved over to Kowloon and we must have been bored so a fellow team mate (who shall remain nameless!) decided to spice up the training a little. The area was in the flight path for Kai Tak airport and every minute or so these massive jumbo jets would come thundering in overhead. He thought it would be a great idea if he launched the balls into the air to try and hit the planes as they taxied in. The next thing you knew someone else would shout 'here's a Quantas Airways' or a 'Cathay Pacific coming in' and he'd start firing these balls high into the sky. We were like a bunch of kids falling about the ground laughing at this totally irresponsible behaviour. I pictured the pilot maybe sitting there with his headphones on, picking his nose and flicking a switch here and there when a Mitre 5 cracks off his cockpit and he's clenching his fist at the window shouting down to us 'bloody kids!' The mind also ran riot imagining passengers preparing themselves for the landing and these balls whizzing past their windows thinking 'What the f . . .' That's how professional we were at Sing Tao.

There were a few ex-Bristol City lads out there and they introduced me to another guy from Bristol who was a school teacher. His name was Steve Jordan and I used to meet him after training and we'd go up to the King's Head pub where they had a happy hour on till eight o'clock. Whilst out there I also caught up with an old acquaintance from my days at Dundee United.

Ian Ballantyne had joined United in 1979 and spent a few months there before moving on to Raith Rovers. He'd been out in Hong Kong for years and had played for quite a few of the clubs, which was fairly common practice among the ex-pats. The flat which Simon and I had been staying in was a bit of a dive so I approached William, who was the English-speaking go-between at the club, and told him I was moving in with Bally and his girlfriend Shelley. They lived in a luxurious government flat in the Sha Tin District north of Kowloon.

At the time, anyone who worked for the government only paid eight per cent of their earnings to live in one of these flats. Shelley's father was the Chief of Police in Hong Kong but had recently taken up a post working for the Sultan in Oman and she had followed in her father's footsteps and joined the police. Thankfully, Sing Tao agreed to my move and paid my share of the rent and I had some right laughs and carry-ons with Bally.

It took a while for me to get accustomed to the ways of Hong Kong and Chinese culture and I remember one time Bally and I were standing on a platform in a station waiting for a train to arrive. I was positioned close to the edge when this train came hurtling in. I noticed Bally out of the corner of my eye, retreat behind me a few paces and wondered what he was up to. His reason soon became apparent when I realised this thing wasn't stopping and the smell which followed a second or two later nearly decked me. I turned round to see my mate doubled over with laughter. 'Oh yeah, I meant to tell you Ralph, that was the transport train for the pigs!'

The standard of football wasn't great but the lifestyle was fantastic. I remember the British Royal Marines came out to the island and we played them in a friendly then joined them afterwards in the NAAFI (Navy, Army and Air Force Institutes) for a slap-up meal and refreshments. I got chatting to a few of them and asked if they knew Tim the PTI who'd trained the Charlton lads a few years previously. They did and said he was off working elsewhere.

One of the biggest surprises I had during my time out there was when I was walking along the street one morning and the front page headline of the South China Morning Post caught my eye – 'SUPERSTAR COMING OUT TO HONG

KONG – FRANK MCAVENNIE'. I think his career had begun to nosedive and he maybe needed a break away from the spotlight and all the off-field publicity he was getting. At the time I was drinking in a pub called Mad Dogs where all the staff were Scottish and a lot of Rangers fans made it their local. I never paid for a drink any time I was in there. When they heard McAvennie was coming out they told me to bring him in and they'd see him all right. 'What, so you lot can rip the pish out of him?' I said, but they genuinely did want to give him some Scottish hospitality.

When we eventually met I just burst out laughing. It was a definite case of 'what the hell are you doing here?' kind of thing from both of us. I said, 'Macca, I've got a freebie for you on the Saturday.'

He'd come over to play for South China and had brought his girlfriend Jenny Blyth (of page three fame) with him so when I told him of the offer from the staff and punters in the Mad Dogs he said, 'What about her (Jenny)?'

'Give her some dough and tell her to go shopping.'

There were two Mad Dogs pubs in Hong Kong and the one we were going to was on Hong Kong Island. I took him in and introduced him to everyone (not that he needed intro-ducing!) then we settled down to a couple of beers. Understandably, the main topic from the punters concerned Celtic and Rangers and Macca gleefully indulged in some stories from the past. We'd gone into the pub at ten in the morning and scooped steadily throughout the day till around six or seven in the evening.

'C'mon,' I said, 'I'll take you up to Lan Kwai Fong. It's a famous area in central Hong Kong crammed with bars.' We went into a bar where I knew the barmaid. What she used to do with me was, if a bill came to $1,000, she'd only charge $100. She didn't know Macca and, meanwhile, he's ordering up loads of booze. On the Sunday I went back up to Mad Dogs and the manager pulled me. He said, 'Ralph, don't bring him back in here again!'

'What do you mean?' I protested. 'You invited him here.'

'He started ordering *everybody* in the place drinks and said *you* were signing for it!'

One of the barmaids was new and didn't know the crack and had just been serving up the rounds. The poor girl was nearly given the sack. I pulled Macca up later and asked him what the hell he'd been playing at.

'You said it was a freezer.'

'Yeah but I didn't say to take the piss did I? You owe me one mate!'

He never lasted long though and I think he ended up back at Celtic.

Going back to the hairy moment in Bar San Francisco, I'll enlighten you of the scary situation in which I found myself one Sunday evening. I'd gotten to know one of the barmaids in there and often popped in for a few beers as it was popular with Europeans and ex-pats alike. On this occasion I'd been out all day and was steaming by the time I sauntered in. The place was fairly small and the bar had a U-shaped set-up so I plonked myself down at the end of the U which meant I was facing the entrance. I ordered up a beer and spent some time chatting to Bona the barmaid when I noticed two Chinese guys entering. This wasn't unknown but it also wasn't a particularly common sight either and I watched as they walked around the bar passing behind me then take up two seats to my left. Both of them were smartly dressed in suits but I nearly shit a brick when I saw what looked like an Uzi sub machine gun protruding from one of their jackets. There was definitely no attempt to cover it up and I began to feel a trifle uneasy.

It's when moments such as these occur that drink wears off quicker than the pattern on a pole-dancer's thong who's been using a pole covered in sandpaper! All sorts of thoughts ran through my head and I briefly considered just making a run for the door. Although I was still fast on my feet I wasn't going to beat a bullet if the shit hit the fan. Alarm bells really started to ring when another few Chinese guys came in and stood opposite the first two then engaged in some heated dialogue with them. 'What the fuck's going down here?' I thought. I shouted up a Carlsberg and didn't dare eyeball anyone. All I wanted to do was slowly sink to my hands and knees and crawl ever so quietly out the door while they sorted out whatever business they had to.

They stayed in the bar for about ten minutes which felt more like ten hours before first, the two guys then the others, upped and left. I was left shaken and well and truly stirred by what I had just seen. 'Bona, I'll have another Carlsberg please!' Later, I was told they were in fact Triads in for a little show of strength but the nature of their business or what the dispute was about was never revealed, which was fine by me.

As Christmas approached a few of us spoke to the club about travelling back to the UK and spending some time with our families. They refused at first but, after arguing that we didn't have any games for a while, they reluctantly gave in and said we could have ten days. The rest of the lads booked up with Qantas, which had a brief stop-over in Bangkok. I opted for Malaysian Airlines which worked out a little cheaper plus it also went via Kuala Lumpur, which I had never visited before. The fact that this deal was an eighteen-day return mattered not – I was going!

It was great to get back to Bristol and see Lee and Robert. Spending Christmas with them was very special but my mind also drifted up to Dundee and thoughts of my elder boy Bradley as well. It was an emotionally tough time. I was able to see in the New Year and the extended break did me the world of good, although I didn't think the Sing Tao officials would view my actions too favourably.

Lee had bought me an expensive rig-out of new clothes and shoes for Christmas so I packed it all in with my belongings and said goodbye to her and Robert then travelled up to London for the return flight. I made sure I was a good few hours early as some of my mates from Bristol were coming up to see me off and have a couple of pints. A couple of pints my arse! I was absolutely steaming! I never even said 'cheerio' to them, I just staggered away with my bag to board the flight. Once we were up in the air the stewardess came around, 'Would you like a drink sir?'

'That'll do nicely. I'll have a couple of bottles of red wine please (only the little ones mind!).' I downed them then crashed out. Nearly six hours later I awoke and wondered where the hell I was. I couldn't have been much company for those around me and probably snored for the duration like a dumper truck. When I did gather my senses I felt brand new again.

Colin Walsh from Charlton once said, 'See you Ralph, you've got the best recovery rate of anyone I know.' I'm not sure if that was a compliment or not but I do think he was jealous of it when he was suffering badly with a hangover himself.

The plane touched down in Kuala Lumpur and I went to collect my case. When I booked the flight I made sure I'd be spending a night in Kuala Lumpur on the return. This back-fired badly, however, when the authorities told me I couldn't get my baggage as it was continuing on the journey to Hong Kong. I stood there arguing and telling them all I had was the bare essentials in my toilet bag but it was no use. There was nothing else for it but to grab a quick wash in my hotel then hit the hot spots in town. I was just topping up the levels from earlier and ended up guttered again.

At 7.30am the next morning I was up and away. We touched down in Hong Kong and I went to collect my holdall only to find that someone had rifled it and taken a load of my gear. I went right off my nut and eventually they compen-sated me so I dropped the bags off and headed straight for a pint in the King's Head. Paul Murray found me in there later and told me the club were going off their heads wondering where I was. Each passing morning they'd ask the lads, 'Where Milay, where Milay?' (They had some diffi-culty pronouncing my name.) Eventually, I had to go in and face the music but it was all a bit of a misunderstanding on my part I said.

I played out the rest of the season and we finished some-thing like fifth in the League but my mind was made up well before the end – I was jacking it in after the final match. The chairman offered me another year's contract but I very politely declined. I had enjoyed life in Hong Kong immensely but there were more important factors to consider. When I moved to Charlton and things didn't work out between Kim and me, I missed out on Bradley growing up and I didn't want the same happening with Robert. The bottom line was I was homesick and needed to get back home to be with Lee and my son.

When I did return to Bristol I found myself in the exact same situation I had when Man United had cut me loose only this time I knew my football career was definitely over, well give or take three weeks!

18

PULLING PINTS AND WURZEL NIGHTS

Some weeks later I received another phone call, this time it was my old buddy Scott McGarvey who asked me what I was up to.

'Bugger all,' I said.

'Right, get yourself fit and get over to Derry City as quick as you can. I'm trying to get the job here. Oh and remember, don't mention your religion.'

'Do you think I'm fuckin' daft?'

I flew over to Northern Ireland and was pleasantly surprised to find a few professional players of note at the club. Ex-Watford legend Luther Blissett was there, as were Neil McNab (ex-Man City among others) and Paul Kinnaird from Dundee United. In the short period I was out there we had some right carry-ons. The team were part-timers and only trained on Tuesday and Thursday evenings. Once training was done what else was there to do? Go fishing? I had to fill my week up somehow and it didn't take long before everyone in The Metro Bar was involved in the game 'spoof', and that included the barman. I was flying back and forth but after about the third week the club had had enough. They simply couldn't sustain the finances needed for me to travel and so another door closed. It was to be the final door and my boots were hung up for good.

I suppose at thirty-two years of age many would consider this to be fairly young. In truth, the mileage I'd covered over the years and the injuries sustained, not to mention the abuse I'd subjected my body to, had all contributed to my career ending in this way. My heart had gone out of football some time ago and when that happens there is only ever going to be one outcome. I never had the slightest intention even when I was enjoying my football of ever staying in the game in any shape or form. Once again I was faced with the question of what to do with my future. I had no plans mapped out, no money put aside and no idea really about how I was going to support Lee and Robert. One option I had was to bury my head in the sand and, for a while, that's exactly what I did.

In the October of 1993 I went back up to Dundee with a couple of mates for a short visit and found my dad was struggling with his health. I took him out for a few pints in the Ferry but I just knew he wasn't keeping well at all. As we travelled back down south I said to my mates, 'I can see me being back in Dundee for a funeral next year.' My prophetic words came true when my dad passed away peacefully at the end of March that following year. It was a sore one to take. I loved my dad dearly (as I did my mum) and regarded him as my best pal as well as my Old Man. Indeed, I thought he would be on this planet forever because dads are indestructible aren't they?

Lee and I eventually got a house in the town of Nailsea, south west of Bristol, and it was there I got friendly with a guy called Roger who ran the Queen's Head pub. It was a real no-frills drinking man's joint which, quite by chance, offered me the opportunity of helping out behind the bar. Some folk may say that wouldn't be the wisest career move to make but I did it all the same! I'd already done a couple of shifts beforehand when Roger approached me and asked if I'd lend a hand on the Sunday of a Bank Holiday weekend.

'Where can I get one of those large plastic bins?' he said.

'You'll get one in the DIY store,' I replied.

'Right, you're on the sangria.'

'What the hell are you on about?' I asked.

'I'm having a "summer theme day". I'm going to paint palm trees on the walls and I've got a ton of sand getting delivered,' he explained.

He was a bit of a character, slightly impulsive and every-thing was typically planned last-minute. His palm trees bore coconuts that hung upside down, a detail not missed by the heaving mass of revellers who turned up later to soak up the sun, sea and sangria (or maybe it was *just* the sangria!). Three young women were 'hired' to wear bikinis for a couple of hours with the offer of free drink all day, which they had no hesitation in doing. I set to work on the sangria and poured just about everything into it. The words 'liquid dynamite' spring to mind!

It wasn't until I was fully committed to helping Roger that he explained I would be working the bar alone, starting at twelve midday. The place soon got mobbed and I was left scrambling on one of the steepest learning curves I've ever known. It was definitely a case of sink or swim. Thankfully, I swam and the bar took in a fortune, but it certainly made me realise just how stressful life can be on the 'other side'.

I had passed my baptism of fire so then that was me in the

pub game. A few weeks later Roger told me he was going on holiday to Cuba with his wife and he wanted me to look after the bar. I thought he was taking the piss but he wasn't.

'You haven't even shown me how to work the cellar and what the gas levels should be etc.'

'I don't have time for all that,' he exclaimed. While he was away I was on the phone to the brewers and others for help when things went wrong. It was another steep learning curve but I got there. Before he left I told him to remember and get his passport stamped in Cuba. Three weeks later he returned and when he came into the pub he made straight for me and said, 'You ya bastard!' then started ranting and raving.

'Hold it there,' I said, 'the pub's been absolutely fine and all the money's up to date and banked.'

'Fuckin' stamp my passport?' he raged. I then realised what he was on about and asked him if he'd got it done.

'Did I fuck get it done? I said to the guy at the desk, "You stamp?"

"No stamp."

I tried again, "You stamp my passport?"

"No stamp, no stamp."

The third time I demanded it he pulled his gun on me and said, "No stamp, this not America!"'

I'd wound Roger right up before he'd gone and I was pissing myself laughing by now just imagining the comical scene at the airport.

He told me he and his wife had gone on a sightseeing tour when the bus broke down in the middle of nowhere. Everyone was informed that they must remain on the bus but he was having none of it so he said he needed a toilet. He popped into this dilapidated shack and ended up drinking with the locals while everyone else waited patiently for the bus to be repaired. He was a belter. He kindly let me stay upstairs in the pub for a period when I was going through a hard time at home. I'd been going out at nine in the morning and not getting home till nine at night pissed and something had to give.

There was a mobile caravan parked round the back of the pub which an Italian guy who worked at the restaurant up the road lived in. I turned up at the pub on Boxing Day morning to find the thing completely gutted and part of the pub also damaged by fire. The Italian lad disappeared and was never seen around these parts again. The guy who came up to carry out the repair work was someone I knew from Bristol and he told me he wanted to buy the pub from Roger. A deal was struck and I began working for him. After about a year things went sour and I was sacked. The parting gift I received was a beautiful black eye! It didn't stop me drinking there and six weeks later I approached the owner and told him I was taking my name off the license as I was officially still the licensee. The pub was dying a death and I asked him if that's what he really wanted.

'Meet me tomorrow,' he said.

The following day he sacked the guy he'd brought in and gave me my job back. Once I settled in again I began to bring bands in and the place used to be packed. At that time Nailsea had a dozen or so boozers so there was a fair bit of competition to get the punters in. I had a guy called Billy Wicks who used to come in and do a tribute to the legendary Adge Cutler.

Adge was the founding member of the Wurzels who'd had massive success during the mid-70s with classic songs like 'Combine Harvester' and 'I am a Cider Drinker'. Adge was tragically killed in a car accident in 1974 but the band carried his legacy on, topping the UK charts in 1976. They'd gained a huge following in their native Somerset and used to play in a pub just up the road from the Queen's Head called The Royal Oak Inn. When Billy broke into songs such as 'Drink Up Thy Cider' the punters would be up on the tables going mental. They were great nights.

I was making a small fortune for the owners who then, incredibly, sacked me again. I thought, 'What the hell's going on here?' They were in the process of going through a marriage break-up and the guy's wife decided to take on the pub after the split. She gave my job to a so-called mate but after a year or so she pulled me up and asked me what was happening (to the pub). I didn't quite understand what she was getting at until she said, 'Well when you were running the show we were making money and now I'm not and haven't done for the last year!'

'Well, doesn't that tell you something?' I said.

Her employee had allegedly been filling himself and plenty others in the bar with free drink. She asked me to come back and, being a glutton for punishment, I took up the post for a third time. One Monday morning I was working away doing my ordering and buying of stock when a mate from Bristol popped in. He asked if I still had contact numbers for my ex-Bristol City team mates, which I did. A good friend of his had been tragically killed in a road accident and he wondered if it would be possible to organise some kind of charity match with the proceeds going towards his friend's widow and their kids. I told him to leave it with me. Twenty minutes later the phone went and a bloke comes on asking, 'Hi, is that Ralph Milne?'

'Speaking,' I answered.

'My name's Neil Forsyth and I'm from Broughty Ferry.'

'Yes?'

'Well, we're all in London,' he said.

'Who do you mean *we*?' I asked.

'There's a load of us down here who support Dundee United and we have a supporters club called the South London Tangerines. We'd like to come down to Bristol if possible and play a game then the plan is to head down to Plymouth and catch up with Paul Sturrock.'

At first I thought it was a wind-up by someone at the capers but it was dead genuine so I set up a match for them to play against the ex-City players. After the game we all went back to the Queen's Head for a fund-raising auction and some refreshments. I explained to Neil that half the money was going to my friend's family and the other half was going to Ninewells Hospital in Dundee, but the London lads very generously agreed to give their half to the widow and her kids, which was a fantastic gesture. He reasoned that it would give them the opportunity to come back on another occasion.

One of their players, Fraser, had a Dundee United top with him which he put up for auction. He then paid £100 to buy it back and gave it to my son Robert. What more can you say to that? Again, it was a fabulous gesture. At the end of it all the event raised over £1,000, which was a great effort for a small pub. The night was tremendous but most memorable was the moment when one of the SLT mob was returning from the bar with a tray of about fourteen drinks when someone banged into him and he dropped the lot. He just about turned, went back to the bar and said, 'Can I have the same again please?' It was hilarious. That then was the start of a bond which I've kept with the South London Tangerines.

My relationship with Lee sadly came to an end after ten years. We weren't getting along and it was unfair to prolong the negative atmosphere which was darkening the family environment. Lee was a special woman with whom I'd spent a large part of my life and who had given me a beautiful son. We had some great times together but, unfortunately, we had to go our separate ways.

The SLT guys came down again, this time for my fortieth birthday, and I managed to organise a match at Bristol City's ground Ashton Gate against the City Supporters Club. My mate Alistair ran a pub just outside Nailsea called The Battleaxes and we went back there afterwards for a right shindig.

Alistair was originally from Stirling and another guy, Frank, who I became friendly with, hailed from the same town. He was an ex-member of the Black Watch regiment and on one particular occasion he invited me to the local TA army barracks to join in their Burns Supper celebrations. Unfortunately, the troops got deployed to the Gulf just before it was due to take place and Frank was left with no option but to cancel. I approached Alistair and said, 'Let's go ahead with it anyway, we'll do it ourselves and hold it in The Battleaxes.' Within a week or two we had it all organised and planned to show our English friends just what it was all about.

We hired full kilt outfits and sold all the tickets for what was a highly anticipated event. Alistair said he'd like to get the local press involved so I made contact with one of the papers and told them the story. The guy asked if it was me who was organising it and I said, 'No, it was my friend

Alistair Scott.' I thought for a second then added, 'Its Alistair Scott McTavish.' A few days later he was having a pint in the Queen's Head when his wife phoned the pub and informed him he should go and get a copy of the paper. He came back in calling me all the bastards under the sun for giving him the surname McTavish, but we had a right laugh!

On the morning of the Supper I told Alistair I was going for a couple of pints then I'd be back in the afternoon for a few hours' kip before the festivities kicked off proper in the evening. However, my 'couple' turned into twelve and I was somewhat gassed when I stotted into his bar. Just as I told him I was going for a sleep, the phone went and I heard him saying 'Fuck off, you're winding me up!' When he put it down he said, 'That was Skinner saying HTV are coming down to do a live piece for television this evening. He must think I'm daft!'

Before you could say 'boo' three big HTV lorries had pulled up outside the pub and began unloading their equipment. I turned to him and said, 'Right, I'll be seeing you, I'm off for my kip.' This went down like a ton of bricks and he protested that I couldn't possibly leave him to deal with all of this. I stopped one of the TV guys and asked him what time we'd be going on air. 'We're going to close the programme at five-to seven with you guys.' As it was still only mid-afternoon his statement was music to my ears and I headed off for a much-needed kip. Our big TV appearance went without a hitch and the evening that followed was a huge success, so much so that we did another five or six of them.

I met up with the South London Tangerines again when they invited me up to their place to present their football team's Player of the Year award. They were very kind and generously paid for myself and my girlfriend to travel up and stay in a hotel. We had a marvellous time and I took up some of my old Dundee United shirts, which the lads had great pleasure in donning for personal photographs.

Life in Nailsea had begun to lose its appeal though and I felt more and more of a pull towards my home city of Dundee. I'd often gone back for visits, usually no more than a week at a time, but in early January of 2005 I decided to spend a fortnight there. Many times I'd hinted to family and friends that I'd like to come back to Dundee and settle once more but I'd always gone back down south. This occasion was different, however, and a lot of what got me thinking had to do with my mum, who had not been keeping very well at all.

When I set eyes on her my decision was made. I didn't really have anything to go back to Nailsea for. My son Robert was with his mum Lee and we had by then been separated for some years. I did return briefly, but in the March I gathered all my belongings and left for good. Eighteen years had passed since I'd left Dundee United for Charlton but I knew deep down that one day I'd come back. I'd made many, many friends during my years spent down south, but it felt great to be back in my 'proper' home.

For six months during 2006, my mum was in a ward for terminally ill patients in Ninewells Hospital, although she wasn't terminally ill. The powers that be just couldn't find a place for her in a care home. One day I was pushing her along in a wheelchair and she told me to get her out of there. She said she had the money to pay for the care she required, which by then was full-time. I kicked up hell with the authorities but the only one we could get her was down in Arbroath. She was adamant she was going to Broughty Ferry but in the end she had to go to Arbroath and we reassured her that travelling down was not an issue for us. On the Christmas Eve morning of that year I received a phone call on my mobile from my sister Linda which I missed. When I called back I said, 'This isn't the call I've been expecting is it?'

'I'm afraid it is Ralph, she hasn't got long to go.'

It was strange really, I got out of bed and my mum always insisted I was clean shaven so I tidied myself up and phoned my sister to tell her I'd pick her up on the way. Unfortunately, we only got to the outskirts of Arbroath when we received the news that she'd passed away. I was devastated. My mum (just like my dad) was a pal as well as a parent, a real special woman whom I thought the world of. Time, they say, is a great healer but as the days turn to months then years, my feelings of hurt and loss remain as strong as they ever were and I miss them both dearly.

19

WANNA BET?

I make no excuses when I say that drinking alcohol and gambling have been two self-destructive vices which I've been fighting a constant battle against for a large part of my life. There's no denying that both have affected me personally, emotionally and professionally in some way or another over the years but the truth is I enjoy them. I'd hate to try and put a figure on the money I've spent on both over the years but the word 'obscene' springs to mind.

It's hard to put my finger on when the gambling took a hold but I guess it was around sixteen years old when I began to take a serious interest in punting on the horses. I think the problem was you won a few quid and you thought you were Archie and it just escalated to the point where it gets a hold of you. Over the course I've put on some shocking bets and lost but, then again, I've had some good winners. It's the same story for anyone who gambles. When you add drink to the equation the buzz becomes greater but so too does the risk factor. Arguably, the more drink you've had, the harder it becomes to acknowledge a sensible cut-off point and cut your losses on a bad day.

When I was with Dundee United none of the other players

were really interested in the gambling. It was just something I got into myself and I enjoyed it. I remember one occasion when I was still young and a United player (who shall remain nameless) placed a bet along with me after I received a tip on a certain horse. We both put £40 on at a price of 8-1. It strolled home and we very nearly cleaned the little bookies out. Back then I didn't place any heavy bets for the simple reason I didn't have the money, but the trips to the bookies were frequent to say the least and this carried on when I moved to the other clubs.

I recall my first 'big' bet when I was at Bristol City, which was £100. It might not sound much now but back in the late 80s it was a fair whack to just go chucking on a horse. I was earning a decent wage but not one where I could justify that sort of betting. At the end of that day at Taunton, after numerous bets I was still up £150 and over the moon. The friend I'd gone with owned a bookies shop and he'd lifted ten grand on the same horse on which I'd placed the £100. He gave me £100 and said, 'Ralph, go and get two bottles of champagne and I'll join you in a minute.'

There were five or six people and I overheard them saying that they owned the horse which my mate had won big on and they were asking each other who had won the sizeable bet. I said, 'Oh that was my mate.' When he came back up to the tent I told him I'd been chatting away to them and that you'd won. He went right off his rocker. 'You don't tell *them* that!' he bawled. 'It was *their own* fuckin' jockey who gave me the tip!'

I thought to myself, 'This is a great game to get into, what with all the inside knowledge,' but it doesn't always quite work out like that. The same friend took me to 'Glorious Goodwood', set in the rolling green hills of the Sussex Downs, but I lost £200 that day and was gutted. I didn't know a hell of a lot about the horses I was betting on but I remember one called 'Oh So Mellow' ridden by the great Lester Piggott which was second favourite; it was a beautiful horse. It romped home at 4-1 but, unfortunately, I'd put a whack on the favourite. It was one of those days.

I had a slightly better time at Royal Ascot one year when I met up with my mate Andy McPhee and some of the Dundee lads. I was still in Bristol when I received a call saying a squad were travelling down and we should get together. The famous meet had been moved to York so I hopped on a train and made the journey up, studying form on the way. I'd singled out a horse and was sure it was going to be a certain winner so I banged a hundred quid on it. It came in at 4-1, the champagne was ordered up and I was off to a great start!

I was pretty successful during the course of Saturday and the bubbly stuff was flowing good style. We were all having a ball. I stuck £500 on another 'certainty' for the last race which was priced at 6 4 and as it stormed into the home straight I made my way to the bar and ordered up two bottles of champagne. It crossed the line in first place and Andy turned to me and said, 'You're fuckin' bonkers! You had that champagne ordered before it was anywhere near the line!'

I just smiled and said, 'I knew it would win. Here, get a glass of this down your neck.' At the end of the day we staggered out of the racecourse to find the longest taxi queue in the world. 'Fuck this, we're not waiting here,' said Andy. He had a quick scan of the area and found an alternative means of transport for us – a beautiful white stretch limo. 'Take us into town Jeeves!'

The guy asked what name we were under. It wasn't the one he was after and we were unceremoniously bundled out in front of the watching masses who thought this was hilarious. We had the last laugh though when we noticed a flat back lorry parked nearby. We approached the driver (who had this bloody great Rottweiler dog sitting next to him) and asked if he'd take us into town. He'd be paid well for his trouble. Before he had time to change his mind we stumbled aboard and told him to 'step on it'. Just as we departed, we gave the crowd a rousing rendition of La Marseillaise for our French friends who had just gubbed England at rugby! Afterwards, one of my mates did a rough tally and reckoned I'd bought somewhere in the region of thirty bottles of champagne over the weekend and I still ended up with £1,500 in my pocket. It was crazy.

When I signed for Man United I was earning a bit more money so I began punting bigger sums. I won somewhere in the region of ten grand over a period of six weeks and I thought I was the top man in town. It didn't take the bookies long to get their money back, however. I was sitting in a pub pissed with Norman Whiteside and Paul McGrath and I phoned up the bookies to place a bet on a horse. My limit for a single bet was £500 but because they knew I had ten grand I was allowed to place a bet for three grand on this horse. It came in third. My mate, who was a bookmaker, called me for everything when he found out what I'd done. He said, 'You could have bought that horse and trained it for a year for three grand – it's a fuckin' donkey!' That outlined the dangers of being pissed and betting, but I was oblivious.

I used to go to Haydock all the time with my mate, which was only twenty minutes away. I would always punt heavy there and we'd drink the best of champagne. On one occasion we both lifted ten grand and had been downing champagne all day, buying for one and all to help us celebrate our successes. By the time I'd got back to my local, The Grapes in Prestwich, I was steaming but carried on with the champagne binge. When I awoke in the morning I couldn't find my money and began to panic big time. It took a while before I came to my senses and remembered I'd posed it safely – nearly too safely! This practice of hiding money was one I used regularly when the amount was substantial but there was always a chance of it backfiring and not being able to find it again, especially when drink was involved.

Lee came with me once to Haydock, just to experience the whole 'day at the races' thing and see what all the fuss was about. The more involved in the gambling game you got, the more people you were able to call on for some inside tips. These didn't always work out favourably but when they did it was fantastic. Anyway, prior to going along I contacted a friend in Bristol to ask if there was anyone I could approach for a good tip. All he could advise was a good horse which was running in the last race and going into it I was three grand down. The horse was priced at 6-4 favourite and I asked for two grand on it, but they wouldn't take it. I had to see my contact. Thankfully, I got hold of him and he took the bet. The only problem was the price started fluctuating like crazy and not in the way I would have wanted. I thought, 'You've shot yourself in the foot big style here Ralphie boy!'

The horse came in at 5-2 and the guy gave me it at that price, which he wasn't supposed to. I was now laughing. I phoned my mate in Bristol and told him of my win then asked him what I should do. 'Buy him a case of champagne and send it on to him,' which I did. Basically, it was a fiddle but I wasn't caring, I was on cloud nine! Days like these were brilliant of course, but the bad ones far outweighed the good lifts. I suppose when you're in this game it's the age-old problem of not quitting when you're ahead.

20

REFLECTIONS

As the years roll on towards my fiftieth birthday I look back on my life and career and wonder just where the hell the time went. Writing this book has certainly given me cause to dig deep inside myself and search every little corner of my mind in order to tell this story. I have tried to tell it as honestly and accurately as I can, however, like anyone else who has ever told their story, there are certain elements which, for personal reasons, have remained in the shadows. I am no different from any other human being and have made my fair share of mistakes while following what has been, at times, a bumpy path. That same path, though, has also afforded me some truly wonderful experiences, the kind of which only a select few ever have the pleasure in tasting. For the people who helped me get there, I am eternally grateful.

As a little nine-year-old Douglas lad I didn't realise just what the significance of my actions would be when five mates and I travelled across town to Charleston for trials with Dundee Celtic Boys Club Under-11s. We won the match 9-4 and I scored five. That was it; I signed for them and embarked on a magical journey through Sunday Boys football winning all sorts of trophies and medals along the way. With manager Bill Donaldson at the helm and some dedicated people helping out in the background we just went from strength to strength and developed into a cracking little outfit.

Although I was one of the youngest members of the squad, I learned quickly and together we all just got better and better. I owe a huge debt to Bill and guys like Paul Hegarty and Paul Sturrock who would spend their free time giving us invaluable coaching sessions. I still have warm memories of travelling on two buses with my mate over to St Columba's school in Downfield for training. I remember in particular a guy called Brian Rankin who played briefly for Dundee United getting on the bus. He asked us, 'Do you know where St Columba's school is lads?'

'Yes, we're heading up there ourselves,' we replied.

'Where's your training kit?'

'We've got it on under our clothes!'

These were the days before fancy holdalls, shiny flashy ultra-modern kits and Bend-it-like-Beckham's £130 boots. We had a T-shirt under our jumper, shorts under our jeans and a pair of battered old sannies (sandshoes) and that was us set!

Those were great days, then to go on and sign as a professional for Dundee United, well that was just the stuff of dreams. I have an abundance of personal highlights during my career with United, but the ones I'd place at the top of the pile would have to be scoring the winning goal for the Under-16s youth team in a tournament in Dunkirk, scoring on my debut against Dunfermline and then scoring a twenty-five yard rocket against Celtic on my Premier League debut which made me the youngest player at that time (eighteen years old) to score in the Premier.

Up there also are the times I scored against Dundee, which was just about every time we played them! And taking part in my first European tie in the UEFA Cup against Anderlecht at Tannadice. Another highlight (although I never took part in the game) was the return of that tie in Belgium and seeing Frankie Kopel's screamer nearly burst the net. In fact, all of the European ties I played in hold great memories, but easily the best one is the 4-0 destruction of Standard Liege at Tannadice in the European Cup.

Predictably, my all-time favourite has to be scoring at Dens Park on the final day of the season on 14 May 1983 to help Dundee United win the League. For a local boy to score for his local team against our greatest rivals on *their* turf and pick up a League-winning medal on the same day is just *Roy Of The Rovers* stuff really. I still have to pinch myself yet. Never in my wildest dreams could I have imagined such a finale!

The United fans always gave me a lift, especially on the big occasions and European nights. It was almost as if you had to match their enthusiasm with your own performance, which I suppose is how it should be. When I look back at the goals I scored, many of them were considered by onlookers to be 'spectacular'. I must say there's no better feeling than catching a ball sweetly and watching it rattle into the net. I never scored many inside the six-yard box – that was Luggy and Doddsy's domain, but every team needs players like them. Luggy once paid me a great compliment when he said I was one of the best finishers he'd ever seen. That was something coming from a guy as dangerous and lethal as *he* was!

On the flipside of all the happy days were of course the dark days when it all started to break down and I began to get left out of the team. From day one I felt I was under pressure from Jim McLean. I think it all went considerably sour after the European Cup semi-final in Rome. Maybe it was down to the chance I missed, who knows, but the whole experience over there was just terrible and our manager bore the brunt of the Italians' vile behaviour. There's no question we had a clash of personalities and this really came to the fore during my last two years with United, which I thought were horrible. I got the feeling he was saying to me 'you're not good enough' yet I was still able to score goals at the highest levels in Europe.

Without doubt it affected me psychologically. I felt suppressed at times and this led to some totally negative behaviour. I often think what might have happened had I walked out on him when I was younger but I decided to stand my ground which, I suppose, was what he wanted. It seemed like a bit of reverse psychology and for a time it worked as I performed at my very best. In the end though, we parted company and nobody won. I think we both lost out and so did Dundee United.

On a positive note, Jim McLean was, and always will be, a United legend, and rightly so. What he achieved for the club was phenomenal. Technically, it was frightening what he came out with. He was a true perfectionist in every sense of the word. I would go as far as to say he was obsessed with perfection. That was the benchmark which he set for himself and everyone was expected to follow his example – nothing less would do. Even the slightest thing had to be right, such as a linesman bang in line with play at all times. A yard or two either side of the line and he would let the poor guy know about it.

This may sound strange given the significance of something

so monumental, but I don't know if the League win really satisfied him in the way it should have. I just don't know. It was an incredible accomplishment and the realisation of some twelve hard and dedicated years of building and shaping a team of winners, who could play a bit as well. He was the top man when it came to footballing matters. If you were a purist you could listen to him all day talking about football and if you had an argument, you wouldn't win it. I've still not won it!

I think Wee Jim would be the first to agree that he had an exceptionally talented squad of players. However, it was he who hand-picked them, brought them together and blended them into one of the most exciting attacking teams of the late 70s and early 80s, and that's not taking anything away from the brilliant teams which first preceded then succeeded the League-winning squad. He got the best out of them all and he sure as hell made sure you were fit! If you weren't fit, you were pulled back for another dose of punishment in the afternoon. Quite simply, if it wasn't for Jim McLean, I wouldn't be writing this book.

I didn't want to leave Dundee United but what happened happened and I had to get on with it. The Charlton move was a nightmare. The way they tried to coach people, coming from United to there was like going from high school back to Primary One! No disrespect to the players at Charlton but I did stop and think, 'Fuck me! What have I done?' With my marriage and personal life spiralling out of control, the loan move to Bristol City helped revive me emotionally. When I scored that scorching volley on my debut it brought some of the old fire back and rekindled my love for the game. The move to Manchester United was like the icing on the cake. It doesn't get any better does it? Even though it soured towards the end I can always say I've played for them.

Would I change anything in my life? Probably the only thing I'd change would be my contract with Dundee United. I don't think it's up for a couple more years yet, after which I'll be a free agent at last! Seriously though, there's nothing I would change. How can you? I've had a great life and travelled all over the world doing something I loved doing and playing against some of the best teams and individuals in the game.

In my hometown of Dundee I still get many people approaching me wanting to talk about my days at Dundee United which I find very humbling. I regard myself as one of them, just a normal punter. I don't deny it's nice to still be remembered. I'm just happy that I was able to give something back to them through football.

A couple of large functions were held in 2008 to mark the twenty-fifth anniversary of the League win. Even after all these years it still feels like one big family when I meet up with former team mates. We still keep in touch regularly with each other, continuing what has been a truly unique and special bond. The same year saw the Arabtrust commission a retro remake of the scarf – which they named 'The Ralphie' – that I was snapped holding aloft after we'd won the League at Dens on that historic afternoon. Again it's very humbling to be honoured in such a way. In January 2009 I was inducted into Dundee United's Hall of Fame and what better time to be recognised for your contributions to the club than its centenary year! I felt very honoured and privileged to receive such an accolade and take my place among some of United's true legends of the past.

At the time of writing these last few words I received a letter from my former club informing me of their wish to induct me into Dundee United's 'Team of the Century' at the official centenary celebrations in Dundee's Caird Hall. This great honour most definitely tops the lot. The fact that both the club and supporters have chosen to include me ahead of some outstanding greats who have graced the Tannadice turf fills me with immense pride. It has made the whole journey worthwhile.

'What's it all about Ralphie?'

Well now you know.

EPILOGUE

IN THEIR WORDS

BILL DONALDSON
(Ralph's old manager from Dundee Celtic Boys Club)

Dundee Celtic Boys team was an offshoot of the original Charleston Celtic. As there were too many players in the Charleston team they split and that's how the Celtic Boys came about. They weren't long started when this young lad turned up for a trial one day for the Under-11s. He put in a great performance for one so young and that was to be the beginning of a remarkable relationship between Ralph and Dundee Celtic Boys Club.

He was very loyal and stayed right up until Under-16s. Many managers used to try and poach him with promises of new football boots and the like but he never took them on. The team was very good as a whole but Ralph stood out a mile playing the role of lone striker. Everyone would look to get the ball to him as more often than not he would stick it in the back of the net but there were those very rare occasions when he got snuffed out and we would struggle a little.

I still have my old record book of all the games we played

in and we had always scored in every match in which we took part. Our record was under serious threat though during a Scottish Cup tie at Lochee Park against Hillside when we were trailing 5-0 with only ten minutes remaining. Thankfully those fears were allayed when up popped Ralphie who banged in two. That was one thing I remember about him, he hated losing!

I had a strict rule with the laddies; if they didn't appear a quarter of an hour before the kick-off, they didn't play. One time we were at Drumgeith Park and Ralph hadn't turned up with my watch ticking ever closer to the fifteen minute cut-off point. All the boys were panicking, 'Where's Ralph? Where's Ralph?' He then appeared away at the bottom corner and they were all shouting to him that he wasn't going to make it so he bolted across to us going hell for leather. I told him, 'You just made it by five seconds OK?'

It was good to keep them punctual and on their toes. Another thing I did with them was advise them on their pre-match breakfast, which was scrambled eggs and toast. I met Ralph's father a few years after he'd gone with United and he said, 'So you're the guy responsible for the scrambled eggs and toast?' He was still religiously having it before a big match, which was nice to know.

We once went down to Newcastle on a trip to play Wallsend Boys Club who hadn't been beaten for three years. This was the team the legendary Alan Shearer would later grace through his youth. Their team's assistant was a Scot and he told me their manager had done nothing but brag about how many his team were going to give Celtic Boys. A few of our team had pals (Ralph's mate Andy McPhee being one of them) who'd travelled down with us on the bus and I decided to give them a game. It was a big mistake and we were down 2-0 after twenty minutes. I pulled them off and put the big guns on – Ralph, go get them! He did just that and scored a hat-trick as we gubbed them 5-2. Before he went on he said to me, 'If I score a hat-trick will I get a fish supper?' After scoring the three he shouted over to the line, 'If I score six will I get a double fish supper?' He could be a chancer at times!

We were very lucky back then because Paul Sturrock used to come every week and train the boys. He was great with them. He used to get his dinner at my house every Sunday. It was a great set-up for the boys because the direct link to Tannadice and Jim McLean was there for them if they stood out, and Ralph did, as did a few of the others. There was a lad called Jimmy Carling who was technically better than Ralph but he was a lazy, lazy player and Ralph used to say, 'Get him away from me, I don't want him with me!' He wanted the whole forward line to himself. All he wanted to do was score goals. He was very greedy, which any good striker should be. Technically, he wasn't the best but the pace he had was electric. That was his forte.

I sometimes felt sorry for the lower teams and their managers who turned up week in week out totally dedicated but would occasionally have to go home having suffered an horrendous defeat at the hands of Celtic Boys. We once beat a team 36-0 and Ralph scored something like eighteen of them! He ended up scoring an incredible 500+ goals for Dundee Celtic Boys.

He was a good lad who always trained hard and did what he was told. I never had one bit of bother from him, never a word back from him. He was a character, a definite one-off. Anytime we were away on trips he would keep everyone amused with his piano playing and capering about. When he went to United I was really pleased for him and followed with delight as his career took off.

PAUL HEGARTY
(ex-Dundee United team mate)

Ralph came into the United side as a young player but showed remarkable maturity and confidence on the park and very quickly he settled into what was considered a successful team at the time. He definitely wasn't overawed and soon made his mark, establishing himself as a very important member of the team. It was noticeable from an early stage that this young man was something exceptional and had been gifted with outstanding natural attributes. His pace was lightning and he would stroll past seasoned defenders as if they weren't there.

One of the memorable things for me was his ability to score sensational goals. There's no doubt he was a big-occasion player and Ralph would often produce goals in matches when it mattered most, whether on the European stage or the important domestic games. On top of that, he was very brave and had a fantastic work ethic, tracking back to help his defence when needed.

As team captain there were the odd times when I would have a quiet wee word in his ear but I also received it – we all did, if we needed to 'pull up our socks a little'. Sometimes though it was the opposite and a few words of praise were all that was needed just to say, 'Keep doing what you're doing' kind of thing.

Back then the squad had a unique bond and I would say when we were on the park there were eleven captains out there. We had a fantastic bunch of guys who quite simply enjoyed playing football and I suppose that special team spirit forged us into a real force, one which eventually saw us clinch the Premier League title in 1983. That whole season was undoubtedly Ralph's finest and it's a real shame that we never enjoyed so much more of those incredible displays. I wished he would have taken his career to the next level and gone on to do bigger and better things and entertained people in the way that only he could. It's scary to think if he was playing today just what kind of price tag would be placed on a talent like that.

DAVIE DODDS
(ex-Dundee United team mate)

I can honestly say that Ralph Milne was one of the best uncapped players in Scotland, possibly of all time. Certainly back then there was an abundance of good players challenging for places in the national side but he could play wide, he could play centre forward and he could score goals. He had everything at the time. He was a brilliant finisher and was always confident in his own ability.

Even as a young lad coming into the team I remember the self-confidence and belief he had in himself. For beating players with his pace he was unbelievable. I've had the pleasure of playing alongside some great strikers in my career, such as Ally McCoist, Maurice Johnston and Mark Hateley, and Ralph is right up there with the best of them when it comes to finishing. He was a natural who could score with both feet and nine times out of ten, if he was through one-on-one with a keeper, the ball would end up in the back of the net. His feet were just so quick and for being a mostly wide player his strike rate was phenomenal.

The service I received from Ralph, Eamonn and Luggy made my job a whole lot easier. I would never have scored nearly as many goals as I did for United had it not been for those guys. Ralph and co. did the donkey work if you like and I just had to make sure I was in the right place but we did have a great understanding between us. I would say the only bad thing about playing with speed merchants such as Ralph and the others was that I took a lot of the kickings and punishment because defenders couldn't catch them!

I would describe Ralphie as being a precocious talent. He had the confidence but also a certain amount of arrogance to go with it. He was good but sometimes he thought he was better than good himself, although I do mean that in the nicest possible way. Having said that, Wee Jim knocked a lot of that out of him. Ralph has maybe mentioned at some point during the course of his story how well we as players all got on back then. I would say that was down to Wee Jim who had us all staying more or less within a ten-mile radius of Dundee which meant we could socialise together as a team. It was a great pleasure to play alongside Ralphie.

EAMONN BANNON
(ex-Dundee United team mate)

The only way to describe Ralph Milne as a player was 'exceptionally talented'. These are no doubt words which have been used frequently when talking about him, but that's exactly what he was. I partnered him for the Friday training sessions at United and he always worked extremely hard. I remember the sprint training races between Kevin Gallacher, big John Clark and Ralphie, which were very keenly contested. Personally, I think what put him up above the rest was his ability to score goals. He was a tremendous finisher with both feet and the memorable thing for me was that he could score goals you just wouldn't expect.

Fans on the terraces will recall many great goals he scored but, as players, we were treated to these week in week out on the training ground as well. When you added this to his lightning pace he was a huge asset to have in the team. I suppose we were like two bookends playing on opposite wings. I was trying to copy what he was doing with the ball and, who knows, maybe he was trying to copy what I was doing but, whatever we did, it worked well.

JOHN REILLY
(ex-Dundee United team mate)

I'd say Ralph, along with Davie Dodds and Paul Sturrock, are possibly the three best strikers that ever played for United and it was a privilege for me to be a team mate and to learn from those three. You only have to look at the old video footage to see the number of quality goals Ralphie scored. Left and right foot and also a fair few with that dodgy creased haircut he had! And he never even got capped for Scotland – unbelievable! When you see the figures mentioned for some players in today's transfer market, well you'd think United's loan/debt would be wiped out and more if a player like him was available now.

DAVIE NAREY
(ex-Dundee United team mate)

I think the best way to describe Ralph is extraordinary. On a football field he came into his own and could do things which were just incredible. During my playing days with him, I was fortunate enough to witness some truly breathtaking performances. There was so much more to Ralph than his sensational pace. For a start, playing on the wing was alien to him but he quickly adapted and developed into a formidable winger capable of destroying any defender on his day.

He had ball control, two great feet, a sharp brain and excellent vision and could cross a ball accurately. On top of all that he could score goals that were out of this world. Whether it was with the head, left foot or right foot, he was the complete package. The goal he scored against our city rivals Dundee on the last day of the campaign in 1983 was a piece of footballing brilliance.

We were so lucky to have such a squad of guys who were all highly skilful individuals in their own right but who pulled together to form an unbreakable team spirit. Aside from the football Ralphie had a healthy sense of humour and enjoyed a good laugh but he was also intelligent and focused when he needed to be. Great memories indeed.

JOHN CLARK
(ex-Dundee United team mate)

I was only a young lad when I came into the team and Ralph, like many of the others, made a big impression on me. He was one of the boys, a real man's man who enjoyed a laugh and a bit of fun but on the pitch he was totally focused. His pace and ability were amazing but he also had the knack of scoring really important goals when it mattered most. His goal against Dundee (14 May 1983) was just pure genius and I think that epitomises Ralph Milne the football player – an unbelievable talent.

NORMAN WHITESIDE
(ex-Manchester United team mate)

I remember Ralph joined Man United at a time when there was still quite a drinking culture. In particular, Big McGrath (Paul), Robbo (Bryan Robson) and me were involved in this and enjoyed the odd beer or two. I got to know Ralph early doors as he shared the peg next to me in the dressing room and it didn't take long for him to join our little social gang. We used to drink in a pub called The Pomona Palace which at the time was one of the dingiest, scruffiest boozers in Manchester. There were some right sessions carried out in that joint! Ralph called it the 'Eighty Club' simply because it used to cost him about eighty quid when he was drinking with us, which was a fair amount of money back then (late 80s/early 90s).

I remember organising the club's Christmas night out for

the lads and took the whole of the first team to the Palace. I was still on crutches due to a knee injury and hobbled about sorting everyone out. A few of the lads were not amused at all with my choice of venue while the rest of us got guttered. They just couldn't believe we were holding our big night out of the year in there but for McGrath, Ralph and me, this was *the* place to be! I would often kid him on in the dressing room the morning after a heavy session and tell him I was sure he'd drunk a bottle of aftershave before arriving. Ralph was a really nice guy though and I got on brilliantly with him.

JOHN HOLT
(ex-Dundee United team mate)

As a player Ralph was very lucky to be gifted with such exceptional pace. Added to that, he was a real opportunist when it came to goalscoring as he proved on so many occasions. More often than not they were spectacular efforts from distance which he could strike with both feet. Personally, I think the team which enjoyed so much success during the late 70s and early 80s was down to manager Jim McLean's ability to spot and develop talent at a young age. His scouting network managed to dig out and nurture many local boys such as Ralph and mould them into formidable players. In truth, we were like a big family. Heggie (Paul Hegarty) once said if he'd ever had to endure the hell of the trenches during the War he'd have surrounded himself with his trusted team mates. That's how close we were.

RALPH MILNE, 11 September 2009

Exactly forty-four years ago to the day, Dundee United destroyed their bitter rivals Dundee 5-0 on their home turf of Dens Park. I was only four years old when Finn Dossing, Dennis Gillespie & co. ran amok and had their names etched forever in United's folklore. How apt then it was for the club to organise their official centenary celebrations on this historical date in the city's Caird Hall. As I mentioned earlier I was informed of my inclusion in Dundee United's 'Team of the Century' a month or so previous to this monumental event and I must admit it was somewhat overwhelming.

As a young lad playing football for Dundee Celtic Boys, never in my wildest dreams could I have imagined where this path would lead me. Never for one moment, even as an adult, did I ever think I would receive an honour such as this from my former club. Adrenaline rushed through my body as I heard my name announced. It was my turn to walk onto the stage in front of a capacity crowd and receive my induction into United's greatest ever team. It was all very humbling and hugely emotional for a boy from the Douglas housing scheme to be recognised in his own city by his local club.

I only wish that my parents Mabel and George Milne could have been in that crowd along with my sons and family members to witness me receive such a tremendous accolade. I'm sure they would have been the proudest parents in the world.

The fans as always were fantastic and again, it is very humbling to think that they still hold me in such high esteem. When I think back on how lucky I have been to be part of the finest era in the club's history as a former player, I think it is extremely important to remember and appreciate the fans who turned up week in week out (and still do!) to support the club. I find it incredible that these same people still want to stop me in the street and talk about the football and how much it meant to them, which is why I knew it was such an honour to be included in the 'Team of the Century'. In my opinion it seals the view of how good a player I was (without blowing my own trumpet!).

When you read the history books and think of all the great players who have donned the Dundee United shirt over the past 100 years, I find it very hard to put into words just how good it feels to be part of the eleven. This night matches any of my great memories from the past and will stay with me forever.

I would like to dedicate this award to my two sons Bradley and Robert.

With love, Dad.